Effective Interrogation

Naxalism–Police–Intelligence

Attention Authors

Manas Publications is fighting a war to tell the world that India can win the battle not only by the bullet but also by pen. We are converting fighters into writers. There is no dearth of intellectuals in our country, however, their knowledge is confined to them only. No sincere effort has been made by any other publisher to channelise their knowledge, which is why the talent of every intellectual remains latent. An author always presents the raw material in the shape of a manuscript and it is the job of the publisher to convert it to a finished product. Manas has been continually motivating intellectuals and publishing their manuscripts for more than two decades and would like to publish your manuscript too. If you or your colleagues have a manuscript ready for publication or are working on it, contact us with a detailed synopsis and list of contents. Manas will also suggest you a suitable title for writing related to your area of expertise. Manas is known for its publishing quality. We take utmost care in publishing and also give wide publicity to the book and its author through our national and international distribution network.

Effective Interrogation

Naxalism–Police–Intelligence

Gadadhar Chatterjee
Former Intelligence Officer,
India

Manas Publications
(We Convert Fighters into Writers)
New Delhi-110002 (INDIA)

MANAS PUBLICATIONS
(We Convert Fighters into Writers)
(Publishers, Library Suppliers, Importers & Exporters)
4402/5-A, Ansari Road (Opp. HDFC Bank)
Darya Ganj, New Delhi - 110 002 (India)
Phones: Off.: 011-23260783, 23265523, Res.: 011-23842660
E-mail: manaspublications@gmail.com
manaspublications@yahoo.com
Website: www.manaspublications.in

Impression 2015

ISBN : 978-81-7049-375-4

Rs. 595/-

Designed at
Manas Publications

Printed in India at
RK Print Services, Delhi
and published by Mrs Suman Lata for
Manas Publications, 4402/5-A,
Ansari Road, (Opp HDFC Bank),
Darya Ganj, New Delhi - 110002 (INDIA)

Contents

Preface

Desire to write a comprehensive book on interrogation tradecraft incubated in my mind during my tenure in the soil of Kashmir (1990-1995). Interactions with several police and paramilitary formations further ignited this tempo. Posting in the Intelligence Bureau's Central Training School at New Delhi provided me further scope to study, in depth, the theoretical aspect. The service and opportunity provided by the library of this school needs special mention. Post retirement engagement as a training facilitator intensified my interaction scope with different segments of trainees. It became clear that interrogation to elicit information could retain its position in police investigation. The demand of the trainees for relevant study materials and paucity of the same, encouraged me to write this book.

Interrogation is a challenging task and an unending process. Escalation of "high voltage crimes" and inculcation of more sophistication has increased the demand for trained hands. My long standing field experience, total dedication in the process and the inculcated faculty could be traced from the elaborations preferred. Obviously I paid total respect to the official oath and commitment to my appointment. However, proper attention has been paid to cover required aspects. Focus has been mounted to touch the field requirement of the day and as such additions of few burning topics. Interrogators should have basic knowledge about the crime contour vis-a-vis the national crime scenario. Updating of knowledge and inquisitiveness are reckoning factors.

I had to draw a line of limit to control the fatness of this book. If it comes as a real aid to the interrogators, my labour and long years of stress would be priced. I bestow special gratitude to those authors whom I have consulted and further tender apology for not soliciting individual acknowledgement. The publications which helped me immensely, a chart of those has been appended at the end of the book.

Grateful to Aruna, my wife, for her generosity in allowing me to serve in trouble torn Kashmir. Frankly, the experience gained there was priceless.

I have only tried to introduce the subject, thus solicit comments from the readers.

Gadadhar Chatterjee

Introduction

Gone are the days when interrogation used to be the synonym to torture and inhuman treatments. Fortunately this long perceived practice has been wiped away with the interference of the Human Rights (HR) and alike bodies and also with the advent of new techniques. The contours of interrogation underwent significant change with the introduction of scientific and technical aids. Spurt of terrorist activities, prominence of the under-ground operators and transnational links have further added sophistication and geared up its importance. The ordeal of interrogation is not a modern concept. From the very dawn of human civilization this methodology has been in use. The group Chiefs, Clan Heads, Rajas, Kings and Sultans relied upon this system in order to ascertain the truth and factual details. The procedure was, however, cruel. Methods, approaches and techniques too were orthodox. The purpose of such suo-moto interrogations was aimed to inflict punishment and also to set an example to others. Curbing of crime and also to project administration's supremacy were other cardinal objects. It was rarely a skilled area. Another goal was to elicit intelligence. In most of the cases, the subject in order to save himself from bearing inhuman and lethal torture, even when innocent used to admit guilt. Gruesome torture, extraction of organs and causing grievous injuries were very common actions spearheaded by the interrogators. Selection of interrogators used to be tough posture and hard mental make up.

Indian democracy has done away with these measures and the Constitution itself has incorporated adequate provisions. Several Articles not only ensured safety and security but also notably restrain few actions. The consideration to treat innocent till guilt is proved, not to compel anyone to witness against himself are few governing codes which further consolidate the democratic fabric of the country. Both the natural and civil rights of the citizens have been equally protected. Interrogation is an important process of criminal investigation. Indian courts, however, till date do not fully rely or give absolute cognizance to the Interrogation Reports. Criminal justice system of the country is somewhat stringent but impartial in their pronouncements. Thus the benefit of any doubt always goes in favour of the accused. Demand for hard, authenticated and conclusive proofs are required factors.

Interrogation is one of the most trusted, reliable, tested and pivotal source for the collection of criminal evidence and intelligence. It is considered as the best, well-sought-after method and the keystone of a successful investigation. It is primarily aimed to search or dig out the truth, confirming or denying involvement in an offence, a rapport, suspicion or alike charges. It may be kept in mind that the interrogee may not go scot free if his complicity is proved. Interrogation helps in developing, knitting and culminating a case and is only a pre-requisite for the collection of evidence, eliciting clues for fresh arrests and also arrest of the absconders, making recoveries and finally for the preparation of a well versed document. It also helps in exposing nexus, networking, targets, both covert and overt activities, command structure, arms holding, memberships, gang composition and leadership, area of operation, strength and weaknesses, modus operandi and funding. Their connections and contacts in the administrative, police, judiciary and political circles together with their intelligence networking could also be elicited. The total picture emerging out of interrogation may not match the initial thinking layer of the interrogators. Many covert information concerning both the crime and the perpetrators is also ascertained through it. In fact, the dictum is, "There is no last word in interrogation".

The success of an interrogation depends on the energy, inquisitiveness, imagination, knowledge base, anticipation and drive of the interrogators. During the course of interrogation many non-serious, roundabout and connected inputs emerge, which if further persuaded, may be of vital importance. The process may also embark from "known to unknown and vice versa". There are many illustrious instances of solving pending or even closed cases, with the half of information casually obtained from the subject. Fundamental point is the anticipation, openness and innovativeness of the interrogators. Long and detailed persuasions and seriousness are also the chords. Inputs can even be garnered from "unconnected" subject. Alertness is, thus, another key, besides training, experience and efficiency.

Interrogation is a fact-finding mission. By FACTS we mean and include :

- F- Find out the fact
- A- Analyze the fact
- C- Check the fact
- T- Test the fact
- S- Summarize the fact

Interrogation is a process to disintegrate facts from concoctions, deceptions, manipulation, dodging and dragging. Elimination, corroboration, anticipation and examination are thus to be systematically and effectively carried out. No imagination is to be there. The golden principle of interrogation is, "Listen more and talk less". It is prudent to allow the subject to open himself and let him speak what all he is desirous to elaborate. The more he speaks, the chance of mistakes or covering up are more Only aspect the interrogators must keep in mind is that the fault-lines may be noted and in the process those may be questioned and re-questioned.

By LISTEN we include

- L- Learn from the uttering
- I- Instigate him to reveal
- S- Systematic and steady approach
- T- Tracking of the mind
- E- Eroding of all the blocks/hindrances
- N- Nexus establishment

Listening, thus, is an important grid in this game. Attitude, feeling, thinking, proper mental framing, personality, experience, education level, status and deceptiveness could easily be gauged if the initial revelations made by the interrogee are minutely watched. In sizing up and rapport building process proper listening plays a significant role.

Centrifugal focal point of any interrogation is to create an urge in the mind of the interrogee. Human nature rests upon creating a wall against revealing the truth at the very outset specially where his own involvement or complicity remains. The punishment factor too provokes him to adopt deceptiveness. There are, of course, few individuals who can withstand the punishment and so accept the guilt. Credit goes to those interrogators who can create an impulse in the mind of the subject early to come out with the truth. To bring the subject on the right track and establish a good rapport are of paramount importance. Since both the interrogee and the interrogator are human being, psychology plays a pivotal role. Knowledge, experience and study govern the scene. The difference remains with the authority and command. The interrogators derive their authority authorized by the law codes while the interrogee too harbour a lot of protection both from the natural justice as well as from national and international laws. The Constitution of India and the rulings promulgated by the Courts, HR bodies as watchdog, are significant factors, putting pressure on the interrogators. Human consideration, therefore, would be the check and balance. Human approach and treatment are expected norms. Each interrogation and each interrogee may be different. There may be few commonalities but the tradecraft yardstick shall never be the same. It is really a battle of wits. The success or failure shall rest upon the technical knowhow, knowledge, approach, experience and total tackling of the subject. It is a psy-war, a psychological game, an open field where the success shall depend upon the nursing of the sensory chords. Deceptions, dodging and de-dodging are the expected behaviour pattern of this game. Talent and toughness together with firm determination are thus pivotal characteristics the interrogators should have.

The major obstruction, however, emanates from the subject. Reasons are many. Wooden attitude, pre-conceived ideas, fear, past experience, threats pronounced by the group members, family compulsion, social status and indoctrination are few forces responsible for the promotion of deceptive attitude. On the contrary, interrogators should be void from any pre-conceived idea, pressure or compulsion, rather they should be of free mind and be ready to accept any bearings. They need to be innovative, tactful and professionally competent. Their thinking process should be such that they should be ready to accept any eventuality, both positive and negative. Sizing up the subject and studying of his revelations, mood and temper, non-verbal communications and mental framework are essential component of this game.

Crime content and the relevant factors should also be carefully and seriously studied in the preparation stage. Result orientation may consume time. Time and stress are determining factors. Mind that the subject is alone and that too in a confused state of mind while the interrogators are in a team. Command and control remain with them. Environment too is favourable to the interrogators. Time fixing and other adjustments are also in the hands of the interrogators. Difficulty arises when the subject owing to illness or injuries is hospitalized. The subjects of the Counter Intelligence (CI) fields are highly trained and their knowledge in the trade craft field may be extensive than those of the interrogators. Important and difficult natured interrogations like the left wing extremists, religious indoctrinated members, volunteers and fanatics of many hues including the militants and the terrorists require trained hands to tackle them. Dearth of uptodate knowledge, background of the organization, their linkages, modus operandi, pocket of influence and identities are few gap areas which require upgrading. Only trained interrogators need to be summoned and none else.

Interrogation is a specialized art of questioning an unwilling subject in order to create an urge in him through tactful persuasion so that he discloses the concealed truth and provides useful information or inputs. The aim is to create an impulse or simulating the subject to bring him to a point where he would loose his so long projected behaviours and also his deceptive endeavour. Interrogator's tact, technique and persuasions shall ultimately be the winning strings. It is, therefore, a battle of wits and human consideration together with psychological treatment which shall outwit each other. It is necessarily a psywar. Watching minutely the body language, utterings, silent listening are few methodologies. Proper attention to each and every act, at both normal and abnormal, upon which proper focus and attention is required to be paid. The tact and technique of the interrogators specially to rope the subject in his own utterings would help in avoiding tough confrontation.

Reaction and behaviour of the subject too vary from subject to subject. Veteran criminals, highly indoctrinated militants, Fidayeen groups and terrorists are likely to act indifferently than those of the normal criminals. Children, juveniles, drug addicts and mentally deranged subjects require differential treatments. None is expected to reveal the truth at the very outset. Some sort of nursing is essential. Exceptions are very common and unexpected phenomenon. But there are few points of deceptive tendency like total denial of the crime, providing redeemed and repeated reply of the same nature alike a tape recorded version, giving corruptive reply, consuming time to reply, taking the plea of memory loss, frequently taking oath in the name of God, overtly polite in giving reply, use of words after carefully chosen, maintaining cool temper, observance of the situation specially the role and questioning pattern of the interrogators and frequently taking the names of noted politicians and police officials.

In the process of interrogation, planning and preparation phase called "Know thy audience" is a crucial one. One should know forehand whom he is going to interrogate and in which case context. Case details, circumstances of arrest, recoveries made, available group details, organization's background, office records and other feedbacks are necessary for the mental preparation of the interrogators. Identification of the interrogee, his body search, and thorough medical examination should be carried out prior to taking up any interrogation. All the recoveries made must be examined thoroughly and important points noted for questioning and corroboration from the subject. All these are done not only to speed up the process but also to decontrol damage line. In case the subject has been interrogated earlier, his previous IR needs to be consulted. The entire team should be apprised of all these feedbacks and the planning endeavour.

Interrogation is a specialized task. Problems and hindrances are many. Few are unexpected and unanticipated too. Increased workload, paucity of time, proper team consolidation, training and experience are known constraints. Interrogation is not one stroke investigation. Mental consolidation, firm determination and calibre of the interrogators are few most sought-after qualities. Discontinuation and lack of tackling abilities are few negative factors. Interrogators, superior intelligence, command and apt handling of the situation would overcome all the stressed factors.

The subject is expected to react in the manner by which he is approached and treated. Initial communications, observation of the mood, temper, attitude and reactions of the subject are much vital keys to be minutely observed. Initial stage in this game is reckoned to be pivotal. It is prudent to forge personal tie with the subject. Tough attitude, referring the crime contour, linking the subject with the crime and foul words may be avoided at the initial stage. Sizing up the subject and to gain his confidence are initial motive. Juveniles and ladies require separate treatment altogether as well as the victim.

Object of interrogation should be clear to all the interrogators and questioning should be done sequentially and wittingly. Framing, modelling and wording of the questions must have intelligence bearings. Blaming, derogatory, accusatory, filthy words should be avoided in the primary stage. Checks and balance should be there. Intelligent and relevant questions and dialogues get weight.

Normal questions are when, where, what, why, who and how. Questions should never be direct, but round about, presumptive, anticipatory, concocted, situational, relevant and obviously objective. Objective to subjective running is the best procedure. Irrelevant, false, confusing and baseless questions, if required to be put, must be well chalked out and home-work must be done. Direct question forewarn the subject and exposes the intention. It also makes him alert and conscious. Therefore, it is counterproductive as the subject tries to either cover up or avoid replying to such question. Keeping mum i.e. not to pronounce any reply, is another sensitive aspect to watch. Close observation of both his verbal and non-verbal communication modes may provide required answer. Conflicting, overriding and conditional revelations are much critical. All these revelations should be attentively and verbatim noted, questioned and repeatedly confronted till emanation of the correct and acceptable reply. Speech modulation, way of the delivery, time space and volume scale are the watching and monitoring signals to evaluate the revelation made.

Handling of the intoxicated subjects require apt care and caution. The subject remains in a "high" state of mind owing to the influence of liquor or drugs. Normal sense and even strength evaporate owing to sensitization of the sensory organs. Thus normal threats, pressure and feelings do not act to frighten him. Liquor negatively give rise to a daring nature. One negative aspect is loss of self control. Highly intoxicated subject covers certain amount of risk. Another cautionary note is never put an intoxicated subject under any third degree treatment, as the result may be fatal. It is wiser to maintain safe distance from the subject in order to avoid any physical harm. This category of subject, often becomes virulent and aggressive. There should not be any kind of weapons within the reachable or approachable jurisdiction of the subject. He must be kept under constant watch. Similar type of care and caution are to be adopted while tackling mentally unsound subjects. However, provocation is an accepted technique. Provocation would irate the subject and out of fit, he is likely to speak the truth. On the spark of the moment he may reveal the "concealed" truth. He may be allowed to speak and may also be given a long rope. Privacy is a vital aspect. Confidence and privacy should run together. While the subject is in the real revelation stage, in any way, he should not be disturbed. The interrogator who is handling him, never be disturbed too. The subject's proximity with him is viewed as a gain and a matter of credit.

Interrogation is not a new chapter in criminal investigation but with the passage of time, the process and techniques underwent sea change. Gone are the days when third degree used to be the success chord. Now human approach has substituted the third degree method. Verdicts of the Supreme Court and the High Courts, pressure mounted by the Human Rights Organizations and administrative instructions have practically banned any type of third degree or torture, made it a punitive offence. The hands of the interrogators have been tightened. The treatment and dealing should be to a man and not to a prisoner. The concept of treating the subject as a prisoner has got no standing till his guilt is proved. Subject enjoys all rights, be treated as an innocent till his guilt is proved. Brain not muscle is the slogan of the time. Subjects too are abreast of this concept and are not afraid to lodge complaints against the interrogators in case of meting any torture. The Court of Law is also sensitive and allergic over this point. It may be worth to note that by use of third degree methods total truth can rarely be ascertained. The subject in order to evade torture even may accept what all he is asked to be admitted. Thus his untrue version, in the long run, may damage the prospect of the case at the trial stage. Intelligent subjects admit convincing truth and thereby buy time. Once they are in Judicial Custody (JC), they feel free. Partial admission of the guilt is another technique adopted to evade torture. Veteran criminals, terrorists, militants and subversive elements are strong enough to withstand any type of third degree.

Interrogation begins with ideal preparation and ends with the admission of the guilt. Knitting the case and to convince the Court are the set targets. The Counter Intelligence, subjects, foreigners, terrorists and militants run by their "code" names. Thus to establish their real identities at the initial stage is difficult. They also try to dodge by providing documents, of course, fraudulently managed. They are also able to outwit interrogators as they are often trained in the intelligence tradecrafts and are also abreast of Criminal Justice System of the country. Shifting of blames upon others and co-operating with the interrogators are well chalked out tendencies adopted by the subject to buy time and if possible, to save own skin.

Often a question arises whether an interrogator is a negotiator. Straight reply is difficult. Often role of a negotiator helps not only to gain the confidence of the subject but also to establish rapport with him. Damage control is also a part of investigation. Juvenile subjects as well as the rape victims are covered under this scheme. Another beauty of interrogation is to cultivate source. Negotiations do play a pivotal role in this aspect. No negotiation should be carried out without the approval or direction of the authority. The general principles include no promise be committed which you're unable to comply with.

Language is an obstacle. One is able to exchange or express his views properly in the language of which he has got proficiency. Criminals have their own "codes" and "coinages". Their level of understanding is another factor. The questions asked by the interrogators must be well understood by the subject. Proper and effective communication can minimize the "stiff" and "serious" attitude. Using the services of the interpreters are accepted. It is better to have dialogue in one's mother tongue. In some specific cases the Court even orders for the appointment of interpreters.

A very conflicting matter that often creates bickering is drawing up or formulation of strategies in advance. In spite of goodhome work done, only after starting of the process and "sizing up" done, proper evaluation of the subject is possible. Difficult area is when a first time offender without any feedback becomes the subject. Tactful and intelligent interrogators begin with the Part-I of the Interrogation Report primarily to ascertain the background and sizing up the subject. Timing and consistency matter most. It is wise to interrogate the subject as early as possible. He should remain fresh and not disturbed by others. Gravity and importance of the case would be the governing factor. Interrogation once started should prolong till the final outcome. Breaks may be there. It may be in details. There is, of course, no last word in interrogation. Subject's health condition and mental state may buy time. In serious natured cases like terrorists, militants, extremists, CI subjects, transnational operators, etc. at the initial stage i.e. soon after arrest, actionable inputs should be extracted for operational use. Once the arrest is exposed before the press and media, possibility of mismelting of the networking is there. Destruction of evidences, absconding of the co-accused and group members, shifting of arms-ammunition-explosives are likely to be activated.

Lack of co-operation not only at the behest of the subject but often by the victims and eye-witnesses is a matter which requires acute attention. Interrogators should be active to open up the subject i.e. he should be provoked to continue dialogues. It is but natural that none will easily admit his guilt. He will also put his endeavour to save his accomplices or group members. It may also be tough to ascertain the motive. Reliability of the witness matters. Motivated witnesses, persons interested to take revenge and inimical witnesses are dangerous. Tough handling and deep probe should be undertaken in order to arrive at a correct standing. Confidence gaining and proper evaluation at every stage must be carried out.

Accusation is one of the usually adopted plea taken by the subject. In order to express his innocence, the subject tries to persuade that he has been implicated falsely and often takes name of his opponent. He even continues to provide elaborate fabricated revelation in his support and also to implicate others. His accusation to the police may also be his product of deep thinking and afterthought. The interrogators should pay attention to these revelations and then counter. Accusation is otherwise productive as the subject expresses views and cue may be taken from his own utterings.

Attitude is another ignite point in this game. Both the interrogee and interrogators might have their initial attitudinal problems. The endeavour of the interrogee, in the initial stage, remains to adopt a tough attitude with a view to distance himself away from the framed or supposed charges. This dogma may put hindrance in the continuation of the process owing to firm negative attitude. But the attitude of the interrogators counts much. Basically all the interrogators must be firm and determined in their attitude and actions. No casualness be accepted. Their goal centred around breaking the subject and extracting all available information. Slackness or lackadisical attitude on interrogators' behalf is reckoned as "damaging factor". In the confidence building process, professionalism, tactfulness, feeling, sharing and helping might change the mind of the subject. After all he is also a human being and subject to psychological orbitation. Interrogators must be patient listeners.

Aggressive attitude from the very outset better be avoided, rather persuasive method be adopted. Another effective method is to interrogate the subject by each member of the team, turn by turn. Prolonged and unabated questioning, in different ways, may not be sustained equivocally by the subject. He is bound to submit. Subject may also admit a limited or specific or little role played by him in spite of the fact of his total involvement. It is done mainly to avoid hard pressure. Hard criminals, member of the subversive organizations and trained Counter Intelligence subjects do adopt this technique in order to evaluate the knowledge of the interrogators.

Concept of rationalization is a core component in interrogation. It allows the interrogator an opportunity to develop a relationship with the subject. The relationship is of forging understanding and removing the hindrances. The problems, difficulties, turmoil, threat and mental blocks faced by the subject should be well taken. Sharing and caring are permitted. Crime context may be generalized.

Interrogation involves creating confusion in the mind of the subject and thereby even inadvertently extracting truth from the unwilling subject. In fact the subject's mind never remains in a stable state. He also suffers from a lot of odd thinking. He may overtly try to control himself. These psychological contours need to be ascertained by the interrogators who can gradually advance their reasoning to comfort the subject. Subject is likely to be tracked and motivated. Intelligent subjects too adopt "confusion creating technique" in order to twist the case. Their convincing attitude and the projection befool even veteran interrogators. Another technique adopted by the subject in order to buy time is submission of written report. From the face value fabrication is rarely detected. Only when verifications are made falsehood is exposed.

Each interrogation is viewed as a learning experience. The tact, technique, methodology and way differ from case to case.

Even unsuccessful cases are eye-catcher and lesson may be learnt also from these cases. Postmortem of all these cases should minutely be done and the minus points should be discussed.

Proximity and closeness to the subject are the areas connected with rapport building. Rapport means and includes entering into the inner circle of the subject. One must be serious and should measure the subject carefully. Approach should be tailor made, step by step and systematically. Faulty observation, incorrect stepping, lack of attentiveness, visual error and wrong calculations are damaging factors. Conversation ability is the cornerstone of success and sells the ideas smoothly.

Interrogator's calibre should prevail upon the subject and act as a subversive chord. Fear of punishment, social stigma, likelihood of elimination, financial implication, chance of retaliation and fear of embarrassment stress the subject much. All these factors be removed. Psychological analysis, political bickerings, administrative slogs and social conditions may be analysed in perfect ways. It is easy to say but difficult to activate. Needless to mention that lot of patience, experience and professional zeal are required to overcome these stresses.

Gone are the days when interrogation used to be done only by human beings (Police). Gradual introduction and acceptance of Polygraph test, Narco-analysis test, P-300 (Brain mapping), DNA test have altered the scenario. We are even heading towards amending the Indian Evidence Act. Thus both from focus and facts, interrogation process is likely to change its colour and contour. Updating and upgradation of interrogator's knowledge, skill and proficiency are the demand of the day.

1 Interrogation Defined

Interrogation has been defined by several experts in several ways and angles. Few definitions are quoted below :

1. Interrogation is an art of questioning to elicit information from a suspect who is reluctant to part with the information.
2. It is an art and science of extracting concealed information from accused, suspects, terrorists, spies, etc.
3. "To interrogate means to question formally and systematically. The use of the term "interrogate" implies that the effect of the interrogator to gain the information will be restricted by the subject of the interrogation. The subject may be unwilling to part with." [Criminal Investigation Standard. By Joseph Deladurantey and Daniel Sullivan].
4. "Interrogation is a subject about which there is always something new to learn, and it is impossible to lay down a code of rules that will cover all the circumstances that may arise." [George Hathwill, Scotland Yard].
5. Interrogation is talk less, listen more.
6. Interrogation is search for the truth. A yardstick to segregate innocents.
7. It involves a battle of wits, to break the resistance of the subject or suspects.

8. It is a profile source of information collection.
9. There is no last word in interrogation.
10. "The interrogation of suspects is an extension of art in interviewing complainants, victims and witnesses. It is a process of proving and gathering of available data in crime solving." [John. J. Horgan]
11. Interrogation culminates with contest making which leads to recovery, discovery, facts and issues, arrests, clues to collect further evidence.
12. Interrogation is the art that uses proposals and observations to extract the truth.
13. Interrogation is the process of extracting information by examination and cross examination of an individual.
14. Interrogation is the specialized art of questioning an accused or suspect or a reluctant witness, through formal and systematic, incisive or persuasive questions to draw out all facts and circumstances of the case. It is done to elicit desired information from a reluctant person by means of questioning.
15. An interrogation is questioning of a person suspected of having committed an offence or of a person who is reluctant to make a full disclosure of information in his possession which is pertinent to the investigation.

INTERVIEW

During criminal investigations the law enforcing agencies take recourse to both interview and interrogation processes. Though the motive and purpose of these two age-old methods look alike but there are distinctions in techniques, process, scope, utility, authenticity, methodology and systems.

An interview is the questioning of a person who is believed to possess knowledge that is of official interest to the investigator. An interview is basically a conversation between two or more people, on a specific subject, event or incident, with a specific object. Interview is an information gathering process. The questioning may be formal or informal in nature and mainly round about for obtaining first hand knowledge or happening. It shall be factual evidence or even "reported information". In an interview, the interviewee usually offer his self-account of an incident or crime under investigation in his own manner or words. Thus the objects of an interview related to any crime are :

i) Collection or gathering of information: It may be from the site, locality or roundabout areas. The individuals may be eyewitness, or local people. May also be the victim or his family members, friends, associates, shop keepers, etc and

ii) For assessing an individual, a reported crime or an incident or even to verify any unconfirmed report. While conducting verification of any individual this method is often adopted.

Interview is nevertheless a profile source. The reports obtained by this methodology help the investigators to locate, trace, identify and even leads to arrest of the culprits. It also helps in identifying the group or organization involved, and sometimes helps in making significant recoveries. Interview is the face to face controlled conversation mostly by way of informal and systematic questioning of a knowlędgeable person who is willing to cooperate for obtaining factual evidential information relevant to the investigation or about the subject himself. Interviewer should have the quality of a salesman, an actor, ready wits, good understanding and adequate knowledge on human psychology. While in the game he should not air his superiority in any manner but to observe the proceedings carefully and minutely. He should avoid suggesting any answer.

An interview should take place as soon as possible after commissioning of the events. People do preserve fresh memory. Eliciting the truth and gaining confidence of the interviewee are utmost necessary. Normally, there is a tendency among the people to distance themselves away from the police. Selection of right person is another criterion. Before interviewing a witness the investigator should mentally review the case and consider the nature and type of information the person can contribute. He may then easily strike the responsive chord. Interview technique can be improved by training and experience but inherent attitude and thrive are necessary qualifications of a good interviewer. The knowledge on criminals and criminology help in chalking out the plan in a better perspective.

The tackling of the subject is a specialized art. Garrulous witness merely requires initiation. The flow of information has to be channelled towards the required direction. There are people who refuse to part with information. They need to be motivated through neutral/general topics and slowly induced towards the subject.

Victims need to be tackled carefully for their aggrieved state of mind. They should be given patient hearing, be allowed to complete their stories, be permitted to offer their opinions and full fact may be gathered from them which may later be vetted. While interviewing a victim, sympathetic attitude needs to be there but he may neither be supported nor discouraged.

DIFFERENCE BETWEEN INTERVIEW AND INTERROGATION

Interview	*Interrogation*
To gain information.	Testing the information.
In the case of interview the person is usually a volunteer who comes with the information within his knowledge.	The subject may be interested to withhold the information.
Normally held in a friendly atmosphere.	Is done in a hostile environment where the interrogator has an edge.
Revelations flow freely.	Normally structured reply.
Taking note is permissible.	Not recommended.
There is a time frame.	No time limit.
Normally not subject to any pressure.	Pressure tactics may be applied.
Limited to a specific case.	Unlimited hemisphere.
Informally done.	Always formal.
On the spot reliability cannot be checked.	Can be checked.
Non-accusatory.	Accusatory.

contd...

Dialogue.	Monologue.
Guilt unknown.	Guilt known.
No human rights warning.	Rights warnings are there.
Not lengthy.	Usually lengthy.
Unstructured.	Structured.
Planning may not be there.	Well planned.
Purpose is to gather information.	Purpose is to get confession.
Location is varied.	Location is fixed.
Goal is to have a picture, etc.	Goal is to prove the guilt or otherwise.
Attitude and pressure are restricted.	Both could be focused.
Object is not confined to break the subject.	Breaking the subject is the game.

OBJECTIVES AND SCOPE

Interrogation, as popularly ascribed to has got no end. It is an unending chapter in criminal investigation process and endeavour. The objectives are manifold and often, at the initial stage, prognosis is difficult. It differs from case to case, individual and varied upon the organization/group structure and conviction. Each case facilitates learning scope too, including the unsuccessful cases. It is, however, certain that prime focus of interrogation remains orbited with the extraction of truth, elimination of deceptiveness and to collect a complete and composite picture i.e. the total ramification of the case, fixing and confirming the individual's role in the commissioning of the offence and, if possible, obtainment of confession. Further arrests, recoveries, garnering of operational leads and collection of evidences are also essential components.

Scope of interrogation is much wider. In fact, interrogation cannot be limited or narrowed. There is no end of it. A potential subject is a treasure and one can obtain valuable information if properly squeezed. The overt scope of interrogation is an acknowledged and accepted process in criminal investigation through which evidences concerning the case, the subject; his gang / group / organization, etc. could be tactfully extracted. It is in fact a mechanism to elicit or determine the "truth". In this process in a way booking or confirming, and on the other side "innocence" or "not connected individuals" are segregated. The criminal justice system of India is very clear and thus only those whose guilts are proved are taken to task. In this aspect interrogation do play a prominent role.

In knitting or enlarging of the case, interrogation has no little equals. From the fact finding endeavour the range covers ascertaining full details, elimination, unearthing new inputs, developing existing leads, criminal penetration, modus operandi, training and strength, future targets, planning, identity of the leaders and also verifying of available information besides fresh arrests and recoveries. The process also eliminates person arrested upon mistaken identities, acting on false and fabricated reports, and other such malice attempts.

Interrogation can bring a case to a logical end. The estimation of the damage done, target selection purpose and other such covert activities could also be made known. Modus operandi and suspect's connection with the victim are more attractive focal areas vis-à-vis knowledge of the *mensrea* and *corpus delicti* are also extracted. Suppression of crime should top the list. Identifications of the active gangs, their area of operation and strength and weakness, collection of intelligence about crime scenario and cultivation of sources and contacts is also possible through it. Record building, filling up of the missing information and obtaining of a concrete crime scenario of the area are other possible results.

Interrogation is estimation and anticipation. From known to unknown and from unknown to known areas. Intelligent, experienced and skilled interrogators, through their imagination and anticipation, can expand the scope even in blind or dark aspects. Many unsolved or long pending cases have been solved after obtaining clues from "not-connected" subjects. A person being an insider of the criminal world may be having absolute knowledge and even may be privy to many happenings. In a pond not only fishes are cultivated, but there are other varieties of reptiles and insects which automatically grow. Moreover, the beauty of the criminal and antisocial elements lie with the fact that they keep nexus and also monitor the activities, movements and actions of other criminals and even outside operators in their respective areas.

With the advancement of neo-technology, phenomenon growth and introduction of white collar criminals, nexus between the terrorists and the underworld elements, nexus between the criminals, politicians and militants, international patronage and connections, faster and sophisticate communication modes utilization, building up of "pockets of influence", garnering of accurate and action oriented intelligence by the criminals and subversive elements are few growing and alarming areas which possibly further rejuvenate the objectives and scope of interrogation. Now, the battle of wits and the psychological war in order to establish superiority, are matters of estimation and evaluation. Thus the scope of interrogation is better not to be bounded by certain parameter or limit, let it be elastic.

TERMINOLOGIES USED

There are a few terms conception of which is necessary for carrying out smooth and effective interrogation. These terms mainly cover subjects of criminology, sociology, psychology and behavioural sciences. Needless to mention that the interrogators should be adequately familiarized with the correct perspectives and bearings of these words-in-use so that they can infer proper analogy and concept. While fixing the objective bearing of these terminologies are of paramount importance. In this chapter few "terms", their meaning, interpretation, bearing, scope and practical orientation, have been briefly discussed. The idea remained to clear up the ambiguity and to project real conception.

Subject

Subject is the individual, male or female, who is to be interrogated. The term "subject" is used instead of "suspect" on the plea that until guilt is proved, one is supposed to be innocent. If we accept a person as "suspect" prior to the conduct of interrogation and without establishing the charges, it might be a prejudicial and motivated act. Further, all persons, who are to be interrogated, may not always be booked or charge-sheeted. Innocent persons, persons arrested on mistaken identities, arrested on the basis of false or fabricated reports are likely to be set free. Victims, witnesses and other such persons are also the subjects of interrogation. They cannot wisely be called as suspect too. Subject is also called as "interrogee". In interview they are also known as "interviewee".

A subject is normally interrogated to ascertain or for establishing the truth, besides :

- to obtain confession to the crime.
- to induce the subject to make admissions.
- to obtain a clear picture about the fact and the circumstances surrounding a crime.
- to obtain real identity and background of the accomplices.
- to develop a case.
- to make further arrests and recoveries.
- to obtain fresh leads.
- to solve unsolved or pending cases.
- to collect data.

Subject of interrogation may be male, female, juvenile, hermaphrodite, aged person, person of unsound mind and any one connected with the crime. While interrogating a "subject", the level of approach, consideration and dealing shall persistently differ. In interrogation, therefore, subject is the core component and thereby more and accurate focus are needed to evaluate the subject prior to taking up interrogation. The efficiency of an interrogator is gauged on the count of his early entering into the confidence circle of the subject concerned. Subject may be :

- Know-nothing type
- Disinterested type
- Drunken type
- Suspicious type
- Talkative type
- Honest type

- Deceitful type
- Timid
- Egoistic
- Emotional
- High profile
- Well informed
- Economically established
- Religious minded
- Highly educated / Scholar
- Politically well connected
- Highly influential
- Mentally unsound and
- Dutch Uncle i.e. helpful type

Intention

Intention means causing a thing or doing an act, purposefully, with some cogent motive or there should be some design behind it. In interrogation, one of the focused area is to establish the intention of the related case and also about the concerned subject. Commoners do equate motive and intention in the same parlance though there are bit differences. Intention oversteps motive on the count of having an added foresight of the end and acceptance of the action directed towards the end. It involves the means adopted too. Intention includes motive but the sphere is much wider. By criminal intention we mean the purpose or design of doing an act forbidden by the criminal law without just cause or excuse. Intention, whether positive or negative, can be examined or judged from the executed act only. Act includes omission also.

The question is often mooted why so much focus is laid on intention in interrogation. Reasons may vary but if the intention is known forehand, the subject can easily be broken. Early ascertaining of intention also helps in bringing the co-accused under fold.

Common intention implies a pre-arranged plan and acting in concert pursuant of the plan. It comes prior to the commission of the act but the time gap should be narrow. Common intention has been viewed and vetted by the legal luminaries from various angles. It does not mean similar intention of several persons. To constitute a common intention it is necessary that the intention of each one of them be known to the rest of them and shared by them [Tillu Ahir ALL 1949 127]. Common intention may well be developed on the spot between a number of persons, with reference to the fact of the case and circumstances of the situation [Kripal AIR 1954 SC 706]. The existence of common intention implies, though the act has been done by a particular member of team, each member is liable for punishment as if the said act has been committed by him [Nandu Rastogi v. State of Bihar AIR 2002 SC 3443]. Common intention, however, cannot be confused with the same or similar intention. The interrogators, while interrogating a group of persons arrested in a single case, should concentrate and capitalize this angle to rope in the entire circle. Admission or confession of one would normally bind the others.

Modus Operandi

The term modus operandi means plan of working or mode of operation. It further means the particular method or system followed by a criminal or a gang, in order to activate and commissioning of criminal activities. The criminal mind too generates ways and means, rather aptness, which it considers to be most suitable and viable in a particular case. They may go on repeating the same methodology or particular method. The principle underlying this system is that a criminal, like any other human being, is but a creature of habits and is likely to follow the same old method of commissioning crime. Criminals harbour a blind faith and do repeat the earlier successful methodology or technique. It does not confirm that the criminals would never alter or change modus operandi. There was a time when the perpetrators of the crimes were mostly illiterate and thus they were prone to adopt the same tested technique as they used to consider it as a safe, secured and tested method. Tracing of the criminals and detection of the crime were much easier with tracing and developing of the modus operandi. Modus operandi is, therefore, a key to success in any criminal investigation. With the advancement of science and technology and with the extension of neo-criminal fronts like terrorist activities, actions perpetrated by the underworld elements, hawala operations and state sponsored mega crimes, the colour, contours and module of modus operandi too have been radically changed. Crime hemisphere is no more limited to a defined territory. Linkages and nexus have become wide and even trans-national. These are also subjected to radical changes owing to various factors. Criminals too change their habits, ways of life and various other actions and activities either by compulsion or to adjust themselves with changed circumstances. These frequent changes are a challenge to the skill of the investigators. "Route Sheet" or "Modus Operandi Map" may not come to their rescue.

Reference to the modus operandi, in many unsolved cases, may yield positive response. The same method of operation and case histories are bound to lead to the detection and culmination of a case. Professional crimes are much prone to these signals. Modus operandi alone may not be enough end therefore other conjunctive aids may hold good. Modus operandi requires a well organized system of reporting, recording, proper analysis and should be easily retrievable. Investigators should be well informed and be void from any shortcomings. Appropriate utilization on time, is considered as narrowing down the field of investigation as well as saving time. Systematic study of the crime pattern and the modus operandi also help in prevention of the crime.

Ascertaining of the modus operandi is also a task assigned to the interrogators. It helps them in breaking the subject earlier as well as to expose the entire networking. Interrogators should be updated with the Modus Operandi Map of the area concerned as well as of the adjacent areas. Therefore, each interrogator must not only be a trained detective but also must update his knowledge in every aspect of crimes, criminals and their ways of operation. Both the knowledge and experience of the interrogators count much in this process of investigation. The authorities also should hold periodical re-orientation courses in order to enrich and upgrade knowledge, skill and attitude.

Witness

A witness is a person, other than a suspect, who is summoned or requested to provide information concerning an incident, or person, or group, or gang, or about any case or happening. He or she may be a victim, a complainant, an accuser, a source or contact, an eyewitness, an observer, an expert who has examined physical evidence or a custodian of official documents. A witness is normally interviewed but he may also be put to interrogation when he is suspected of lying or withholding pertinent information. While interrogating a witness, the interrogators should know what are the informations to be ascertained or extracted from the subject and what are the expectations in building up of the case. While interrogating a volunteered witness, tough posture may be avoided, rather a compose and comfortable attitude should be projected. Hostile witnesses are matter of concern. Special care should be taken to interview child, woman and senior citizen. Each witness should be examined separately. The important, trustworthy witnesses should be heard first prior to taking up main interrogation to form a complete idea. Interrogators should be cautious about false, malafide and misleading information catered by the witness. Correct study, and understanding the psychology are core components.

Admission

An admission is a self-incriminatory statement by the subject falling short of an acknowledgement of guilt. It is an acknowledgement of a fact or circumstances from which guilt may be inferred. It implicates but does not incriminate. Sec 17 of the Indian Evidence Act has defined an admission as a statement, (oral or documentary or contained in electronic form), which suggests any inference as to any fact in issue or relevant fact and which is made by any of the persons and under any circumstances. Sec 20 further states that statements made by persons to whom a party to the suit has expressly referred for information in reference to a matter in dispute are admissions. Sec 31 of the Act further says that admissions are not conclusive proof of the matters admitted but they may operate as estoppel.

Confessions

A confession is a direct acknowledgement of the truth of the guilty fact as charged or of some essential part of the commission of the criminal act itself. To be admissible, a confession of the accused must be voluntary. Confessions obtained by coercion, threat, physical torture, unlawful influence, by giving false promise to give clemency, offering rewards or benefits, and deprivation of the necessities are not voluntarily made. The subject must be cautioned, prior to making any confession, that these shall go against him and there is no legal compulsion to make confession. The consequences should be cleared to him. Confession is a direct acknowledgement of the truth or part of it. Sec 24 of the Indian Evidence Act says, "A confession made by an accused person is irrelevant in a criminal proceeding if the making of the confession appears to the court to have caused by inducement, threat or promise, having reference to the charge against the accused person, proceeding from a person in authority and sufficient in the opinion of the court, to give the accused person grounds which would appear to him reasonable, for supporting that by making it he would gain any advantage or avoid any evil of a temporal nature in reference to the proceedings against him". Section 26 of the Act states that no confession made by a person while he is in the custody of a police officer, unless it is made in the immediate presence of a Magistrate, shall be proved as against such person.

Depositions

A deposition is the testimony of a witness reduced to writing under oath or affirmation before a person empowered to administer oaths, in answer to interrogators i.e. questioning and cross-examination made by opposite party. A deposition is used ordinarily to take the testimony of a witness who will be at a prohibitive distance from the scene of the trial at the time of the trial. Depositions are taken by the trying courts and not by the police.

Juvenile

According to West Bengal Children Act 1959, child means a person who has not attained the age of eighteen years. The

Juvenile Justice Act 1986 specified the age of a boy who has not attained the age of 16 years and a girl who has not attained the age of 18 years. Whatever might be the age criteria, a juvenile is treated under certain considered views. The role of the police towards juveniles is also somewhat different from that of the adult criminals. The concept of Juvenile Justice System has been conceived by the legislation aiming to provide care, protection, treatment, development and rehabilitation of the delinquent and neglected juveniles. The Constitution of India envisages special status of the Children vide Art 15(3), 24, 39(e) and (f) and 45.

The Juvenile Justice Act 1986 substituted the word "child" (as used in the Children Act 1960) by "juvenile". The two terms, as per the Act harbour identical legal status. In India various Acts and Procedures specified different ages and also treated boys and girls on separate age categories. Few of them are :

Arms Act 1959 - 16 years

Plantation Labour Act 1951 - 12 years

Employment of Children Act 1938 - 15 years

Factories Act 1948 - 14 years

Hindu Minority and Guardianship Act 1956 - 18 years

Indian Contract Act 1872 - 18 years

Immoral Traffic Prevention Act 1956 - 16 for girls

Dr KL Shrimali, the then Education Minister, while introducing the Children Act 1960 in the Rajya Sabha in December 1960 argued for the age of 18 years for the girls owing to social condition of our country though many girls attain their puberty much before. Indian law-makers have always projected their considered and sympathetic attitude towards the children specially upon the neglected lots.

The interrogations of the juvenile subjects deserve special attention and are relatively distinguishable from other categories. It requires a moderate amount of skill. Juveniles may be categorized into two types ; one non-criminal and the other criminal type. Non-criminal types are susceptible to emotions. A friendly appeal and soft treatment may yield good response. Often after the commission of the offence, they suffer from mental trauma and seek supports. Criminal types are rather problematic. Poverty, bad association etc. are few factors which push them in the criminal nexus. Lie is an integral part of their behaviour. They also develop an aggressive posture towards the authorities owing to the utter neglect suffered by them. The interrogators should try to tap the subject by way of putting intelligent questions in an informal manner through friendly chats. Friendly approach should be used throughout. Psychologically moulding the child offenders and creating a similar wavelength matter much in tacking and breaking these category of offenders. These children may not be able to totally express but they often correctly demonstrate the actual happenings or events. Collection of details, therefore, is art in itself. Guardian, family members and friend's help may be taken where applicable. Modern criminological researches uphold the role of the interrogators in reforming the delinquent juveniles. Of course, the role of the interrogators is limited and restricted by the laws. What at most they can employ themselves, are to psychologically mould these young offenders. Often children indulge in childish pranks, fantasies and mostly try to "copy out" the crime witnessed or read by them through media and books. Special care is required to handle traumatized and also violent type delinquents. It is desirable to handle the juvenile offenders by the specially trained investigators

2 Interrogation Tradecraft

INTERROGATION ROOM

Though there is no legally prescribed specification of an interrogation room but here are few accepted norms, and specific requirements to carry out systematic, scientific and uninterrupted interrogations. The room should allow a free process and be void from any interference from daily routine police work. It should be a safe and secured place and there should be a provision for armed guard posting away from the vision range of the interrogee. The place should be distraction free and the doors, windows and ventilators must be closed to plug emission of any noise. Entry to the room must be restricted only to the interrogators even the other policemen should not be allowed. In case of supply of water, etc., these should be served by the interrogator primarily for security reason and secondly to establish rapport. The rooms need to be away from sight and hearing of any undesirables. There must not be any distracting object or view like open windows looking out into outside scenes. Wall hangings are not normally allowed excepting in specific cases, help of maps, charts, etc. may be taken. There should be no telephone in the room. Mobile phones of the interrogators need to be either switched off or be kept in silent mode. Interrogators are not permitted to talk in the presence of the subject.

Modern concept of interrogation room is a combination of both traditional and modern ideas. With the advent and introduction of scientific gadgets and evolution of new techniques, the interrogation room has to be designed accordingly. The room environment and privacy should be within the control and command of the interrogators. Ideally, two rooms in an isolated place with adequate security consideration are suggested. One room to be used for the purpose of interrogation, while the side room is used for documentation, monitoring, observation and meeting purpose. The size and shape of these rooms should have the capacity for laying out table and chair with sufficient movement space for the interrogators. Drinking water, and electricity facilities are must and the toilet must be attached with the room. Toilet room should have only one door and be void from any other ventilations. There should not be any other items, which can be used by the subject to commit suicide. Sound proof room is recommended along with air-condition facilities.

Sitting arrangement in the room requires considered view. Subject is always offered armless chair so that he is deprived of resting and feels uncomfortable, while the interrogators should be provided with comfortable chairs considering the long duration of the process. The chairs and table positioning would be in such a way that these should not create a barrier between the interrogators and the interrogee and must facilitate eye contact facilities. Watching of verbal and non-verbal communication of the subject plays a significant role in this battle of wits. The proximity i.e. the distance between the interrogee and the interrogators plays another important distinction as the truthful and white collar criminals tend to be closer while the deceptive, hardened and die-hard criminals prefer distance from the interrogators. Similar is the case in respect of bully type or human vulture type of interrogators. The sympathetic type of interrogators gain proximity and closeness. Proximity must be adjusted to interrogator's advantage.

Focusing of light on the face of the interrogee is a well known technique. When such light is focused on the face of the interrogee, the interrogators are kept in darkness. The normal lighting arrangements should be such that the eye contact and the body language be studied and also allow normal reading, and other facilities. Light arrangements must be controlled and in case of normal power failure, alternative or stand-by arrangement should be there. However, in this room there should not be any open wiring. Recording of the revelations, at times, pose a serious problem as taking notes in front of the interrogee is considered to be a pitfall of interrogation. Modern technical and electronic recording facilities like Micro Cassette Recorder (MCR), Concealed Cassette Recorder, Wire Bugging, etc. may be used which shall normally not warrant the attention of the interrogee. Concealed Video Cameras (one focused on the face of the interrogee while the others on wide angles to cover the entire proceedings of the room), Two-Way Mirror, Close Circuit TV etc. are few modern gadgets which can be used. The recording, however, is to be carried out in the adjacent room where one interrogator will be deputed, in advance, for recording, listening and analysis. Before installations of these items, the functioning of these gadgets need to be checked. At times, the recorded revelations made by subject's accomplice, may be played as a technique to break or to elicit the truth. Recorded telephone tapping should never be played before the subject as a security guideline. Where the Psychological Stress Evaluator (PSE) or Mark 2 Voice Analyzer is used, necessary statutory precautions need to be observed before exposing these to the interrogee. Whatever and whosoever shall handle these sophisticated items must:.

i) Place the items in advance, prior to entry of the interrogee in the room.

ii) Must have adequate knowledge and experience in handling these items.

iii) After installations, functionings must be carefully checked.

iv) The visual observation of the recording room, must be out of preview of the interrogee.

v) Proper communication channel between the examiner (positioned in the side room) and the interrogators should be prefixed.

vi) All norms of security precautions should be observed.

vii) There must not be any tale-tell mark of these clandestine operations.

viii) The recorded evidences must not be immediately erased or destroyed. It may be produced in a Court as a piece of evidence.

ix) Authorities sanction is a must.

In order to take photograph of the subject, which is a mandatory provision, a camera with accessories must be available in the room. Arrangements for fingerprint, footprint, blood sample, voice recording, specimen hand writing collection, etc. should be readily available. In order to take exact height and weight, to supplement the descriptive role column, a measurement tape and a weighing machine are also desired items in the interrogation room. In many interrogation rooms, the wall marking height scale, is drawn to ascertain correct height of the subject. Necessary transportation facilities must be kept ready in case of sudden physical disorder of the subject who needs to be immediately shifted to nearby hospital. The interrogators should not carry any item, other than the basic requirements to the room, which may evoke any repulsive or otherwise feelings in the mind of the interrogee. Smoking in the room may be avoided.

Interrogator's chair must be higher than those of the interrogee, to project supremacy. Normally they should wear civil dress. The dress code is more important in cases of nervous subjects, women, children and also subjects with a sense to remorse. Tough criminals may be interrogated by uniformed interrogators to make a sense and also to have psychological impact on them. The subjects need not be handcuffed or tighten with rope. However, dreaded and hostile subjects may be treated otherwise. In no case subject be blindfolded. Eye contacts are must. Interrogation Room should look like a modern sitting room rather than a prison or lock up. Relaxed and friendly atmosphere are conducive to carry out the process of investigation. There must not be any handcuff, rope, wanted notice, arms in the room. No object should remain in the room which can be used by the subject as weapon of attack.

In view of gradually escalated demand to interrogate harden criminals not only having inter-state connections but who now have widened up their hemisphere across the border, terrorists already trained in the intelligence tradecraft, foreign agents and other highly motivated and indoctrinated fundamentalist activists, each state should have few marked and standard interrogation centers at their disposal.

SUBJECT OF INTERROGATION

There is no uniform or any set pattern of procedure which can be used on the subjects of interrogation. Reasons are many. The various nature and varieties of crimes, involvement of different groups, organizations, bodies, gravity of the offences, nexus with the national and international outfits, heinousness of the crime committed, motives, jeopardy to national security, are a few offences which are categorized for consideration in the process of interrogation. The subjects are categorized considering, age, sex, psychological order, political status, etc. The subjects may be a first time offender or seasoned criminals, ex-convicts, white collar criminals, trained subversive elements, economic offenders, drug peddlers, immoral traffickers, child abusers (pedophilic), human traffickers, smugglers, petty criminals, border touts, law violators, etc. The subjects may belong to the Islamic fundamentalist organizations, LWE, BODO, Kashmiri Jehadis, SIMI, Al UMMA, ULFA, North East insurgent groups, terrorists, etc. who harbour their individual / organizational commitments. Counter Intelligence suspects, spies, Resident Agents, Hawala operators, Fake currency pumpers, ISI agents, Underworld elements, etc. have got their respective role and motivations. These agents are extensively trained and may be well aware of different interrogation techniques and procedures. The extremist varieties of subjects are well abreast of Human Rights and religious fundamentalists do often take recourse of their religious dogmatism. The political subjects try to influence the interrogators with their political connections. The ordinary criminals too belong to different categories; namely poor who have adopted crime for livelihood, criminals by association, accidental criminals, psychopathic criminals, eve teasers, rapists, white collared, etc. Experience, professional competency, modus operandi and capability to react differ from case to case, subject to subject. There are area-criminals like border touts, guides, couriers, human traffickers, smugglers who mainly operate in the bordering belt. Some subjects also do operate chain wise like drug traffickers, immoral traffickers, hawala operators, couriers, etc. Harbourers are of another kind of subject who only facilitate staying / hiding facilities for shorter duration and often remain unaware of the purpose and identity of the criminals. Their motive may be either money or affiliation. Many a time threat is also used. Islamic fundamentalist organizations mainly use pan-Islamic and religious cards. Some subjects operate trans-nationally. Age, sex, status, education, ethical chords, behavioural pattern, environment, background, occupation, profession, physical composition, mental strength, etc. also varies. Obviously a die-hard criminal would be able to sustain much pressure and a veteran criminal even understand the nature, methodologies and different phases of interrogation. Thus "sizing up" of the subject is a pre-condition for any interrogation. Enough "feedback" would also provide strength to the interrogators to gauge the subject's withstanding capabilities.

In cases of lunatic, mentally deranged, psychosomatic subjects, clinical examinations by an authorized medical specialist is a must. Often the subjects may also adopt this cover to avoid or delay interrogation process. Needless to note that women and children are separate category of subjects who require special handling. Victims of the pedophilic cases are also a separate category and their interview process is significantly different from other subjects. Sick or injured subjects are often interrogated in the hospital ward. In these cases they are kept in segregation and prior to questioning physician's approval and consent are needed.

Language often poses a problem. Hard vocabulary, which is not understood by the subject, may not be used. The questions put should be properly understood by the subject. In the United States, the Miranda Warnings provided the scope to the interrogee even to consult lawyer before answering any question. Presence of lawyers have also been allowed by the Indian courts (Nandini Satpathy's case). There are provisions also to take help of the interpreters. In case a local dialect is spoken by a subject, interrogators acquaintance of the same is a must. In case of a specific code word spelled by a subject, the same needs to be listen properly, then written, with elaboration in English in the bracket. In acute case where the language of the subject is such that interpreter cannot be locally arranged, in such cases the matter may be referred to the Court and then necessary action is taken with the help of the Ministry of Home Affairs and Ministry of External Affairs.

During the process of interrogation necessary care and caution should be taken as per the need mainly to extract truth from the subject. Past handling experience of a similar type and category of subject may help in interrogating a similar type of subject but vouching repetition may not be always a correct judgement. Here comes the scope and effectiveness of sizing up of a subject.

Whoever might be the subject, the focus of interrogation remains on digging out the truth for which breaking of the subject is a must. In this context it may be kept in view that in certain cases, namely the children, the rape victims, the kidnapped persons, other such victims along with the process of interrogation, the interrogators are also employed in damage control measures. Special care needs to be taken against the juvenile offenders. The questioning patterns would necessarily differ as per categorization of the subject. Whosoever might be the subject, the interrogation tradecraft codes shall be applicable to all with necessary variation as per requirement. Thus, the subject is significant and a matter of great potency in the interrogation process. The entire planning and preparation are highly dependent on the potentiality of the subject.

Subjects of interrogation shall also include the following category of persons :

First Time Offender

As the individual is a person entered in the crime scenario for the first time, lack of reference would be there. In rare cases, reference could be collected through criminal intelligence networkings only. This category may further be divided under :

(a) Accidental

(b) By association

(c) Under cohesion, threat or blackmailing

(d) Family/Social compulsion

(e) Motivated by others.

Tackling of the subjects under this category may be easier on account of their lack of experience in sustaining interrogation and bewilderment. Often they come forward towards confession of the guilt but prior to taking any decision, verifications must be made.

Veteran or Professional Subjects

Die-hard criminals and veterans would obviously pose resistance and are likely to be deceptive from the very beginning. Few of them may possess experience of interrogation and even jail experience. Professionals are also trained and highly motivated. They are sure about the nature of punishment and the gravity of the crime committed. These people are, therefore, hard nut to crack. Only experienced, trained and outstanding interrogators would be able to break them. Inexperienced interrogators may be convinced by the acting ability posed by this category of subjects. Bully, human vulture and sneering types of interrogators would be effective to tackle these subjects.

Victims

Interrogation or interview of the victims require apt handling abilities, sound knowledge and experience. Majority of the victims harbour biasness on police as they consider inability and inefficiency of the guardians of law the root cause of their sufferings. Therefore much coolness is required. Better allow them to ventilate their grouse and be normal. Their family members and friends too project non-cooperative tendencies. Soft and human approach are essential. Few victims like rape, children and even senior citizens are much sensitive subjects. Secrecy and damage control are also cogent factors. Victims should never be put to pressure or torture. Sympathetic, School Master and Analytical types of interrogators earn much success.

Youth

Subjects under this age-group are hard to crack. They possess consistency of power and resistance capabilities too. From motivation angle, they are highly indoctrinated and are not normally amiable to any pressure, greed or any agreement. Ideologically subverted subjects under this age-group even dare not to sacrifice their lives for the cause. They have less attachment towards their families too. Youth force, in any society, is reckoned to be the backbone. Tackling and dealing with these subjects require experience and better understandings. In building cover stories and forwarding alibi, they are intelligent and experts. As such more attention and apt-handling are also required.

Aged Subjects

Age old people mainly suffer from poor health conditions, including some chronic problems. Therefore, proper examinations and adequate actions are prescribed norms. Owing to their age, they might have seen enough world and from crime angle might be veteran too. They might also be habituated to take plea of their age and failing memory.

Child or Juvenile Subjects

Laws have prescribed certain procedures in respect of interrogation of juvenile subjects. Few restrictions are also there. Whatever might be the involvement, they require much cautious approach. In no case they may be mentally or physically hurt. Children are the future citizens and to bring them back to the mainstream of the society is the motto of any law enforcing agency. Children are minute observers and can relay the process perceived or acted or demonstrated. Owing to minor age, many may not be able to understand the texture and connotation of the offence committed. They are not to be alarmed about the crime and the punishment factors. Better not to touch upon these topics during interrogation. They, if questioned in a simple and well-understable manner, required and vital information are likely to emerge. They may go for illustration and acting, allow them. One cautionary note is they are easily subjected to be tutored by the guardians and friends (co-accused). Religion and ideology may also act upon them. It would be advisable to interrogate them in their homes and Police station better to be avoided. Their minds may react by observing uniformed police and as such interrogators may be rather in civil dress. No hard, blunt or criminological terms be used. These may create confusion and they may not be able to understand the questions. The victims under this category, both male and female, are much serious subjects and thus require proper planning and preparations prior to the conduct of interview or interrogation.

Women Subjects

Laws and few court rulings have specified guidelines while conducting interrogation of women subjects. In many facets, the hands and proceedings of the interrogators have not only been restricted but in case of any violation, they are liable to suffer the consequences. Women as such should better be interrogated by a lady interrogator or in the presence of a lady. Women victims should normally be interviewed at their places and in the presence of her family or friends. Interrogations of the rape case victims and alike cases, damage control factor, mental consolation and secrecy are to be positively ensured. The provisions of the law should explicitly be adhered to. The sensitivity of the interrogation of the women has been escalated owing to the induction of large womenfolk in terrorist, militant and even in organised criminal gangs.

Hostiled, Disinterested, Mentally Unsound and Threatened Subjects

Subjects of any of these categories need special approach, proper planning and adequate steps as per individual case. It may be wise to confirm whether all the projections, gestures or behaviour on their past are positive or not. Clever and intelligent subject might act accordingly to dodge interrogation. Obtain reports from the medical experts after proper evaluation of the subject. Heavily drunken subjects and drug addicts also, prior to taking up interrogation, may be referred to the authorized medical units for necessary action at their end. Ascertaining the opinion of the authorised physicians and getting them medically treated are the normal prescription which the interrogators should follow.

Deceptive tendencies adopted by the subjects are but natural to evade interrogation and to buy time.

Egoistic Subjects

This category of subjects try to prevail upon the interrogators by projecting their social status, official positions, political rankings and other such positions. They suffer from ego problem. They thus require to be toned up and proper sizing up. Their criminal nexus must be exposed. Tough posture and tackling are the modes. Never subjugate before them.

KINDS OF INTERROGATION

Interrogations are broadly divided into two main heads :

a) Preliminary Interrogation and

b) Detailed or Sustained Interrogation.

Preliminary Interrogation

Preliminary interrogation is the keystone of any interrogation and the success or failure of any subsequent interrogation entirely depends on the outcome of primary interrogation. Beginning from the identification of the arrested individual, his/her involvement in the crime, organization leanings, background and antecedents, family details, etc. are keystone in sizing up, mind-reading, and finally to determine techniques. As this type of interrogation is carried out soon after his/her apprehension, the disturbed and bewildered state of mind of the subject obstruct him/her to build a plausible and convincing cover story. The confused state of mind and the shock are the minus points which the interrogators may capitalize in their favour. Trained and experienced interrogators, thus, deal with the subject in such a way that there remains very little opportunity to play hide and seek game. The material inputs ascertained during this process are useful from feedback point of view and at times remove lot of anticipatory thinking. The further arrests of the accomplices, recovery of the incriminatory items, weapons, explosives, subversive literature and other important items connected with the crime sequence actually depend heavily on the outcome of preliminary interrogation. Damage control such as sequential events, immediate targets, etc. can be foiled, if the details are ascertained during this stage. The inputs obtained during preliminary interrogation, though may have face value but always subjected to verification. Time paucity is a known hindrance of which there is a general complain. The relevancy between the preliminary and detailed interrogations also, in many cases, differs. The importance and significance of preliminary interrogation always remain at a high stake before the authorities. The outcome of this process helps in booking the subject under appropriate sections and provisions of law.The crime record of the subject needs to be checked at this stage in order to ascertain his background and previous crime records, if any. The subject may be arrested in a particular case or even by accident or chance. He may be a highly wanted person elsewhere. His or her photographs should also be flashed through different crime nets including INTERPOL for checking and soliciting feedback from others.

Detailed Interrogation

Indispensable part of any interrogation is detailed interrogation. It is always done by trained and experienced interrogators, in teams, in a controlled atmosphere and in a pre-fixed room. It is a slow, tedious and lengthy process. The purpose remains to extract not only the truth but the optimum possible inputs. The guiding principle is to dig out "concealed portion" and from unknown to known and vice versa. Through this process not only known cases are solved but clues of many pending and unsolved cases are also ascertained. It is the anticipation and knitting experience of the interrogators which are recognized and acknowledgeable factors. The proficiency and expertise of the interrogators are also viewed as success stones. They not only solve the crime in question but also enrich their knowledge on ongoing crime scenario, organization's details, targeting, inner bickering, etc. The interrogators get desired time and thus can prolong their questionings till optimum satisfaction is achieved. This type of interrogation is also termed as a sustained interrogation. Sustained efforts by rotating teams not only minimize the resistance spree of the subject but is also bound to submit or surrender sooner or later. Thus, this process facilitate maximum milking the subject. The system and technicalities of this gameplan act heavily on the psyche of the subject. Obviously the style, approach, techniques, knowledge and experience vary from interrogator to interrogator but the tradecraft knots and guiding principles remain almost static. Variations are, however, permitted keeping the basic requirements of the case. Situational need and subject's mental stigma are also key factors before the interrogators who adopt technique better understood by them, and extract desired inputs. Prime contour of any interrogation is breaking the subject. Checking and rechecking of salient revelations are made. If needed, field enquiries may be discreetly and tactfully conducted without consuming much time. Information covering beyond jurisdiction limit necessarily be shared with the concerned authorities requesting them for early feedback. However, while conducting these enquiries, secrecy of the result must be well guarded since many actions may be depending on it. In this electronic sensitive age, even the criminals have privy to faster communication means and also cleverly use cryptic or code language.

Every details emanated during the process of sustained interrogations should be systematically and chronologically recorded, examined and evaluated by the teams prior to preparation of the final interrogation report (IR). Interrogation per se has got no limit and end. The more the effort, the better the outcome. The area is vast and expandable depending on the subject's position and the drive of the interrogators. In many cases the interrogator who leads the process by putting volley of relevant and intelligent questions synchronizing the intellect and ego of the interrogee, often submit before the knowledge source of the interrogee. Such type of questions help in consolidating relationships too.

Needless to mention that the IR of this kind is always written in a prescribed format. The IR must carry the photographs, fingerprints, footprints, blood sample, specimen handwriting in different known languages, recorded voice, etc. While writing Descriptive Role (DR) of the subject description must be elaborated as per RSHAH + 2 format. More details may be given but RSHAH + 2 is a must.

R = Race

S = Sex

H = Height

A = Age (on date)

H = Hair

Plus two prominent identification marks.

In the "Remark" / "Comment" column, the observation made and noted behaviour pattern of interrogee may be specified. It may be kept in mind that the detailed interrogation report is the subjective version revealed by the subject. The interrogators are deprived of inserting their views or opinions, except in Remark Column at the end.

Detailed interrogations have got the following advantages

- Availability of the feedback about the subject.
- Organization/group background.
- Time for planning and preparations.
- Less mental and physical stress as done by teams.
- Atmospheric advantage.
- Use of technical gadgets including recording facilities.
- Required and adequate techniques be adopted.
- Scope for examinations of each recoveries.
- Cementing of any misunderstanding.
- Enough scope for gaining the confidence of the subject.
- Contact building.
- Missing points may be covered.
- Associate identifications through photographs.

Apart from the above mentioned two types, the following kinds of interrogations are also in vogue :

Screening

Screening is a process of elimination by way of quick interrogation when bulk apprehensions are made. Only the wanted individuals are detained and the rest are normally let off. In search and combing operations many individuals are detained and after screening, by trained interrogators only the suspected individuals are booked. After any alarming incident, the law enforcing agencies encircle the area and start search operation in order to apprehend the culprits. Screening interrogation methodology is adopted by them to identify the offenders. Identification of the culprits is a difficult task. To overcome this crisis, Comprehensive Arrest Technique (CAT) operation is used. This unique process is found very much result oriented, specially in the militant/ subversive activities affected areas. CAT operation is nothing but identification by his own gang/group member who is cultivated by the police and/or intelligence agencies for this purpose. It is a highly sensitive and discreet operation. Professional competency and tactfulness of the interrogators are the sole point of this game. Screening also carried out in and around any vital installations, sensitive offices, defence establishments and in the vicinity of the VVIP visit venues. Resident Agents, Under-Cover Agents, etc. also got eliminated through this process. In the bordering belt and the inter-state boundaries, this process has often paid good dividend to nab criminals of either sides. Planning and preparations are often quick and as such the interrogators must be very careful and attentive otherwise they may be dodged by their adversaries. This process must be conducted in such a way that the popular sentiments of the area people are not touched and it may be wise, if possible, to associate local leaders for proper identifications.

Snap Checking

Snap checking is done with the purpose to detect, and apprehend the deserters, wanted criminals, un-registered foreigners, jail breakers, infiltrators, militants, terrorists, smugglers and other suspected persons. Entry and exit points (port of entry), vehicles, hotels, lodges, guest-houses, railway stations, bus-stands, religious places are the most common places where snap checking are usually carried out by the trained and experienced interrogators with the obvious aim to detect the presence of any undesirable element. It is a recommended process prior to any important foreign dignitary's visit, VVIP's visit, National Festivals, Black Days, National Days, Sensitive Congregations, etc. The adversaries try to outwit the interviewers by solid cover stories, perfect alibi, projecting imitated identity authentication. The adversaries provide solid cover and alibi too. During this process both verbal and non-verbal communications of the subject need to be carefully studied. In case of any suspicion, the subject may be segregated and may be put to further interrogation. Snap checking have foiled many planning of the organized gangs and terrorists targeting owing to sudden and unanticipated snap checking by the intelligent sleuths.

On the Spot Interrogation

Soon after the apprehension of a subject, on the spot interrogation is immediately carried out primarily to confirm the identity of the arrested individual, to obtain details of his/her accomplices, to recover arms, ammunition, explosives, subversive literature and any other incriminating object connected with the crime. In this electronic sensitive age owing to faster communication modes quick actions are recommended. In some cases establishment of the correct identify of the apprehended person may consume time and the person concerned may adopt "delay tactics" by buying time in order to lease out time to his/her associates to escape, destroy the evidences, shifting arms, ammunition and explosives. Use of codenames have posed another significant hindrance. Many of the criminals/militants are known by their pet-names or code-names to their group members and their actual names remain unknown. Frequent change of code names are also common. A sample survey carried out by the writer in Srinagar was significant in which only 27% of the Kashmiri militants could provide the real name of Syed Salahuddin, the then Hizbul Mujahideen (H.M) Supremo. Physical search is compulsory prior to the conduct of this process as many of the dreaded outfit members carry cyanide capsule. They swallow it with a view to deprive the interrogator any sort of information. In the event of any group arrest, identities of the arrested individuals need to be established through this process. Yasin Malik, the JKLF Chief, could escape from Soura Medical College in 1990 as his identity was not established. On-the-spot interrogation found to be acute-result oriented in intercepting communication net-working including human chains, after obtaining details from the apprehended individual. The immediate response of any arrested individual is sporadic as he/she remains engrossed in bewilderness and in a confused state of mind. Defence building, cover story building etc. come at a later stage. The revelations made by the individual must be carefully noted with minute details, and subsequently another action oriented team must act on these. Sharing of inputs beyond jurisdiction may be faster too. The media or any other unauthorized person should not be privy to these revelations/ actions. Plugging of escape routes of the accomplices must be carried out and the senior formations should be intimated. This process of interrogations has yielded positive results in the cases of militants, terrorists, left wing extremists, drug peddlers and underworld elements. These varieties which they spell at the very outset, later on try to deny or contradict. Often they derive support and briefings from their overground supporters, advocates, Human Rights activists and alike elements. At the very initial stage, many subjects fear elimination but when their arrests are confirmed, they gain confidence. An intelligent interrogator often use this technique in his favour in order to dislodge the mental equilibrium of the suspect. The outcome of this process is ever kept under absolute discreetness and the "actionable inputs" should be separately dealt with. During this process personal safety and security of the subject are of prime concern as his/her group members may try to eliminate him/her to plug divulgence and evidential value. The prudence of the killing of Beant Singh, assassin of Mrs. Indira Gandhi, the then Prime Minister of India, is still a matter of debate.

Police Interrogation

In this chapter, the formal and routined interrogations done by the Police mainly at the police station level have been discussed. The focus is on specific crime or law and order related subjects.

These sort of interrogations come under routine police functioning and are mainly investigation oriented. These are voluminous in numbers and tastes alike. Urge, interest and the artificiality act on the ability and proficiency of the interrogators. The scope and utility of such type of interrogations toed only towards the culmination of the cases. The primary focus, attention and angle of questionings, therefore, found restricted towards correlating the offenders and the offence. Material evidence collections became significant. But a professional police officer always thrives towards enriching his knowledge. He pays equal attention not only towards the prosecution but also to understand and study *mensrea*, modus operandi, criminal world, their pockets of influence, strength, leaderships, arms holding and other such related information. The fact that interrogee being an insider, possesses first hand information relating to the events and also a watchdog of the area. The information provided by them has helped solving many unsolved cases and have alerted the police to neutralize many clandestine activities. Cultivation of contacts is another important factor. During the police interrogation, rapport building is found easy. Once won over, the subject may be briefed and trained for collection of intelligence. In this context one very potent need is collection of intelligence about detained criminals in jail may be kept in mind.

Counter Intelligence Interrogations

Counter Intelligence (CI) measures are taken by government to detect, deter and destroy the intelligence operation of a country, both inimical and friendly. The task assigned to any espionage agent is to steal national secrets and to direct hostile clandestine activities against another country. These agents are obviously foreign nationals posted/deployed in our country under both legal and illegal covers. Their jobs center around establishing and escalating intelligence generation networking by cultivating individuals having privy and located at vulnerable and targeted areas. These traitors are Indian nationals. Counter espionage denotes identification, penetration, manipulation, repression, assessment and neutralization of foreign espionage activities.

These operations often resort to espionage, sabotage, subversion, assassination, hijacking, disinformation, disintegration, abetment to terrorism, pumping of fake Indian currencies, drug trafficking, and other such anti-national activities. In this field we get two types of interrogees — one, the Master Agents who are foreign nationals and the second, the Indians, recruited by them. The first category i.e. Master Agents is of two categories. Those who are officially stationed in our country being diplomats and non-diplomats and enjoy protection and immunity under the Geneva Convention. They cannot be tried in our Courts. They can only be made persona-non-grata when their activities are found prejudicial to the interest of our nation. The other types of foreign nationals involved in this gameplan are undercover agents who also carry espionage activities clandestinely. When arrested they are put to sustained interrogations. Major attention is paid to unearth their penetration and damage done. They are also trained in intelligence tradecrafts. In the event of arrest of any foreign nationals in India, both the Ministry of External Affairs and the Ministry of Home Affairs must be informed within 48 hours of their arrests. The MEA, in turn, share the information with the concerned official representative of that very foreign national posted in India. The Second Category of subjects i.e. the Indian nationals arrested in CI operations are of prime consequences. The role played by them is not only stimulating but also embarrassing. Apart from damaging part, it infringes into the very security system. Thus the subjects under this category are always put to interrogations by experts. They do generate many un-known and sensational inputs relating to enemy intelligence networking, area of operation, financial channels, counter-intelligence techniques, modus operandi, penetration, damage done, political line up, agents of influence, subversion, nexus with the extremists, fundamentalist and radical bodies, identification of the Intelligence Officers (IO), key areas of interest, etc.

The interrogation of the CI subjects is a specialized job. These are done only under controlled conditions as the revelations made by them not only act on the functioning of the government but also equally important for harmonious relation with the involved country. Thus utter secrecy is maintained. It is always done in a systematic and chronological way. In each stage evaluation, examination and corroboration of the revelations are discreetly carried out. The State authorities often seek the assistance of the Central Intelligence Agencies for latter's wider vision and ramification. The planning and preparation of this type of interrogation do differ from other types. The CI subjects are highly trained, often persons of position. Even the Senior Defence Services, All India Civil Service Officials, Reputed Businessmen, Senior Political Functionaries, Notable Scientists, etc become the subjects. Intelligence Community is also not free from their targeting net. The very stake and the sovereignty of the nation may, thus, be threatened.

While carrying an interrogation, the interrogators do adopt many techniques primarily to break the subject and finally to extract every details. They keep their focus on two counts to detect the damage done and the deter i.e. to identify the unknown portion. Exposing of the entire networking is also a major thrust. In CI field interrogation is considered a prime source of intelligence generation. Sustained interrogation of one subject often provides many inputs, which are further developed. Videography of the interrogation proceedings are also done mainly to convince the concerned country, if needed. The Interrogation Report is always written in prescribed format and normally treated as classified document.

Counter Militancy Subject's Interrogation

The interrogation of the militants/terrorists/extremists have accentuated greater importance owing to escalation of these activities.

The interrogators should be educated enough to dig out the required information. Every details of any organization's functioning need to be tactfully extracted. Maximum extent of information and leads are the core components. All sensitive disclosers should be fully vetted. Special emphasis should be laid on ascertaining command structure, cells, recruitment, training, targeting, communication channel, funding sources, arms holding, harbourers, overground activists, facilitators, infiltration-exfiltration routes, passport details, national and international nexus, leadership disputes, etc. Putting of questions may be in such a way that no "direct question" is put and the subject is devoid of understanding the source of information. During the process of interrogations help of sketch maps may be useful for easy identification of the place.

As "revenge" is an open method adopted by these groups both the interrogee and the interrogators should be given adequate security coverage. Principle of restrictive security may also be maintained. While interrogating religious fundamentalist subjects, much care and cautions need to be adopted as they are considered to be highly dogmatic and fanatic. They should be tackled and psychological treatment may be given to wipe out the fanatism imbibed in them. Similarly, the left wing extremist subjects are of different category who believe in the radical change in the legally established systems. Their sacrifices, dedications and creating of own pockets of influence should be kept in mind and the planning may be done accordingly. They are mostly educated lot and are also intelligent. Their main focus is on ideas, dogmas and doctrines. Another section, the grass root level cadres, are mainly brainwashed people and economically under privileged. Thus while interrogating subjects under this category, the above mentioned focal points should be kept in mind. The very spirit of the interrogators must be promoted with the motto to win battle of wits. Time, place, techniques and methodologies may be subject to change not the spirit behind. Seriousness, hard approach and drive are thus core components.

TYPES OF INTERROGATORS

The types of interrogators can broadly be categorized in the following manner, keeping sequence with their approach, behaviour pattern, role played, attitude and actions of each interrogator in a particular case, against the interrogee in the process of interrogation. Interrogation is a battle of wits and also a psychological game. Breaking the subject's silence by hook or crook is the cornerstone of this game. Interrogators and the interrogee, both are human beings. Considerate and well orchestrated mood, temper, approach, consideration, feeling and endeavour paid to the interrogation, pay often rich dividend.

Interrogators are born actors and as a professional they develop immense control over their emotions and feelings. During the planning and preparation stage, prior to taking up of any interrogation, anticipating the behaviour pattern of the interrogee and the gravity of the case, interrogating team members decide about the type they would be playing during the process. They do often go for rehearsal. In this context it may be noted that adoption of type may not be essentially a permanent feature, it may be altered and adjusted as per requirement. But each of them must have good knowledge about human behaviour pattern, human psychology, criminology and adjustability. Character study, control over one's own self and control of voice and emotion are also desired norms.

School Master Type

This type of interrogators adopt the role of a schoolmaster and often treat the interrogee as a student. They try to prevail upon by reasoning and counselling. They stress upon by persuasive and counselling methods. They prevail upon the guilt, not on the guilty person and sideline the commitment of the offence as a situational mistake. The prevailing socio-economic conditions, ills of the society, political high-handedness, etc. are elaborately flattered as the root cause. This tactics emote miracle result in the case of emotionally disturbed subjects and also those who suffer from a feeling of remorse. Convincing ability, reading the mindset of the subject, his family and social problems, ego and consolidation of mind are prime consideration elements. Human touch and sympathetic convincing abilities towards the interrogee often soften the mind of the subject and finally subjugate him.

Cool and Analytical Type

Success-wise this type of interrogators claim edge over other types. Perception, calmness, anticipation and analytical approach nevertheless remain the key factors and the contour of any interrogation can even be reverberated. The style and perfectness outwit the subject to read the mind of the interrogators. They never open themselves before the subject. They logically and systematically drive the subject and corner him by winning his confidence and trust. They could connect and knit the revelations and also inflict lukewarm effect on interrogee. The interrogee finally submits himself before the interrogators, as he avails no point of return or deception opportunity.

Sympathetic Type

The polite, friendly, understanding attitude, homely dealing may subvert the mind of any emotionally disturbed interrogee. This type of interrogators are persuasive in nature and could raise mutual sympathy and apathy within a short time. Matured behaviour and awesome handling coupled with gradual ingress upon the subject's mind orient positive result. The rapport and winning the heart by way of blistering sympathy leave no space but to surrender. Thus, this method is purely oriented towards converting the mindset of the opponent. These type of interrogators exploit human consideration and do adopt the technique to subvert the subject. They do prefer congenial atmosphere by breaking official atmosphere. They pay much stress on personal touch, family score, future prospect and often try to convince interrogee towards reasonable consideration for his family members. Educated subjects shall break at an early stage while others may consume time. This type is also known as "Big Brother" type as they play the role of an elder brother. Creating a friendly and harmonious relation do generate closeness in rapport building. Emotional crisis and mental jeopardy need to be carefully studied before hitting the sentiment of the subject. Once nexus is bridged, the interrogators would smoothly break and broach the silence of the subject.

Idiotic Type

The idiotic type of interrogators do spray continuous irrelevant, silly and meaningless questions to the interrogee with a view to irritating him. These questions are purposely put to block the conscious reasoning process of the subject, his free and pre-determined thinking often offgear him. This process also distracts his mind and ego. His concentration gets lost and his defence building also stucked. These sequenceless at random irrelevant infusive questions create such impulse in the mind of the subject and his ego is hurt in such a dimension that he is forced to subjugate himself. Once the subject opens up his mind, he is then gradually brought to confessional stage.

Bully Type

The bully behaviour like shouting at the top of the voice to establish control and authority, thumping the desk, etc. may act heavily on hostile witnesses, suspects belonging to lower section of the society, mentally weak and white collared criminals. This type of interrogators are meant for terrorizing and breaking the nerve of the subjects by their physical postures and verbal communications. They adopt both physical harass technique and hurting the morale by uttering foul and filthy language on the top of their voice. These are also followed by jumps, raining blows, shouts, shrieks, terrorizing and thumping upon the subject. The mood, temper, acting ability, body language, posture of the interrogators, psychologically demoralize and physically subjugate the subject to submit before the interrogators. The seasoned subjects often distance themselves from this type of interrogator. Interrogation is a battle of wits rather than the battle of tongue. But this blustering type of interrogation, at times, produce tremendous results. It has, however, limited impact too. Hardened and trained subjects and even the repeated offenders may sustain this type of interrogations owing to their hard mental make up. In many cases the interrogees in order to save the humiliation, do dodge the interrogators by providing false, incorrect, fabricated information. It helps the other types e.g. School Master Type, to come closer to the subject.

Sneering Type

The technique adopted by this type of interrogators remain in inflicting deep injury in the ego of the subject by sidelining his whatsoever importance. Each individual carry a high image of himself. The interrogators insulate contempt over the subjects by utterances, turning up the nose and through other such non-verbal communications. Egoistic and highly possessive interrogees do break easily by this technique.

Human Vulture Type

The quite, emotionless behaviour, putting questions like a machine create a fear of regression in mind. This type of interrogators spit questions without any emotion, expression and pause in their face. They act like a human machine and only concentrate on their business. They are methodical and considered to be very dangerous type. Their eyes emit anger. The interrogators of this type go in for practising even before taking up interrogation. The facial expressions, body actions/reactions i.e. non-verbal communications of the subject are carefully evaluated by the team. When this type of interrogation is on, one interrogator shall be put to carefully study and note the non-verbal communications of the interrogee. CCTV coverage or concealed cameras may produce effective result in capturing the movements, activities, reactions and other physical modes of the interrogee.

All the types, detailed above, may not be a permanent feature of any interrogation. The proficiency of any interrogator is based on his acting ability, communication skills, perceptions, knowledge, anticipation, command and control, situation tackling, psychological dealing, study of human behaviour, tact in rapport building, confidence, motivation, stamina, determination, experience and overall control over emotion, feelings, biasness and temper. Main focus of interrogation shall be on defusing the subject and to elicit truth as early as possible. In many cases one type may be complementary and supplementary to others. The subject too prefers to be closer to his like-minded interrogator. Interrogation is void of any competition. It is completely a teamwork. Winning the battle is the motto. Thus, team of interrogators should have good understanding, team cohesiveness, perfect training and adjustability.

Time and again the point which remains much potent in the process of interrogation is positioning the subject. Acting ability of an interrogator thus proves to be extremely purposeful though in many times may sound mechanical. This tradecraft is not new. The professionals used to demonstrate which has been now made more scientific and methodical. To train one's actions and activities require more professional approach and training. Needless to note that any qualified interrogator can change the "type" not in a particular case but in different cases. In no case the subject be allowed to expose the typical behaviour pattern or role played by an interrogator.

BASIC PRINCIPLES OF INTERROGATION

Scientific interrogation requires use of mind and brain, not muscles. It is primarily a battle of wits and psy game. Presence of mind, study of the mental, ethical, psychological and physical withstanding of the subject, situational advantage, circumstantial evidences, experience, knowledge are the guiding factors of any interrogation. Interrogation is not a new phenomenon in criminology. In crime investigation, interrogation is an age-old practice. With the passage of time, practice and experience, the following principles have been evolved which need to be carefully adhered to. These basic guidelines are recommended and suggestive in nature. Changes are but natural, depending on the case, situation and subject.

1. Interrogation should be done at a safe, secured and secluded place. It is never done in the house of the interrogee. The reason being subject's home is his castle. The interrogators must have command and control of the interrogation place.
2. It may not be carried in haste. Planning and preparations are must.
3. Prior to taking up any interrogation, detailed background of the interrogee should be minutely studied. Feedback about his group/organization/party and the circumstances of his apprehension must also be ascertained.
4. Fund of patience and confidence are fundamental requisite of the interrogators.
5. Interrogators demand continuity, consistency, determination and creation of superiority complex. These may be done systemically and it must be kept in mind that interrogation has got no end. Therefore, maximum extraction of inputs should be done.

6. Interrogations are done legally and humanly. Application of third degree method is not at all permitted. The subject must not be forced for revelation which may go against him. He must not be given any sort of mental coercion, pressure or threat. Any kind of compulsion or torture should also be avoided. It may be kept in mind that till his guilt is proved, he is entitled to enjoy all rights and privileges as a free citizen in a democratic country.
7. Interrogations should be carried out within unbiased mind and should also be free from any kind of influences. The interrogators should be void of any pre-perceived idea.
8. Classification of the subjects and their status must be obtained before taking up any interrogation. Interrogation process should prolong and development of the common ground for conversation should instinctively be chalked out. To extract the truth is the sole object. Hate the crime not the criminal concept may provide good dividend.
9. Never beg admissions. This approach not only would provide interrogee the upper hand but his mental strength may also be increased. The confrontation should be augmented in such a style that the subject is cornered and his resistance is broken. To break his silence is the core objective.
10. Questions must be well thought of, prepared in advance. No leading question can be preferred. Leading questions not only alert the subject but also quite sensitize him about the purpose of the interrogation. Expert interrogator always put round about questions and try to obtain clues from the revelations made by the interrogee. Questions should be clear, pointed and well understood. As far as possible the questions may be put in the dialect spoken by the subject. Tactics are adopted to put confusing questions obviously to compel the subject the vomit the truth. Cross questionings are must. In fact the art, mode, communication ability, timing and force of the questioning are the powers and strength of an interrogator.
11. Early interrogation is desirable. This process deprives the subject to build cover story. Moreover, at the initial stage

subject suffers from mental trauma and bewilderness. It takes time to overcome the sudden shock. Human memory becomes fainter and fainter with the lapse of time. Criminal justice system also deserves early framing of charges. Delay also may provide scope to the subject to be tutored by others including the advocates.

12. Interrogations are always conducted by trained and experienced police officers. However, in a team fresher may be inducted as an infield trainee. Before his inclusion in the team, he must be adequately briefed about his role in the game.
13. The interrogee should be formally medically examined by the competent physician prior to conduction of interrogation each time. He may also be physically searched each time prior to interrogation.
14. Do not give the subject any false promise. Soft and humane approaches are must but any promise, which cannot be tenable, should not be given.
15. Talk less and listen more. In this technique the interrogee is bound to fall in his own trap. The more he talks, the more clues you may have from his own revelations. If you continue uninterrupted talking, you are liable to divulge many hidden inputs and you are denying scope to the interrogee to express his own words.
16. Frequent interruption may be avoided. He may be allowed to finish what all he wants to speak. Clues may be extracted from his own utterings. It is he who is liable to explain each and every word he utters.
17. Sizing up of the subject is mandatory. This aspect has separately been elaborated.
18. Interrogation is a team work. Thus team spirit, coordination, rotation and interactions are must. There is no rank business or preference in this game. Team must work in unison and without any competitive mood. Credit is shared by teams not by individual. However, if any subject prefers his rapport with any individual interrogator, the latter may be given preference for his closeness to the subject.

19. Never loose temper, patience or be arrogant. At time veteran criminals or trained subjects try to incite the interrogator and distract his mind. Anger is a sign of weakness. Thus one should control his own temper and emotions.
20. There should be no ad hoc approach. Starting from the beginning till culmination and full satisfactory interrogations, utter seriousness is desired.
21. Team members should be refrained from calling each other by names during the process. Even "Sir", etc. should not be used. Team members should also avoid consultation in the presence of the subject. Exposure of the Agency engaged in the interrogation process may also be averted.
22. Interrogators should also be void of any kind of boastings, bluster or insult to even co-interrogator. There may be differences, but open confrontation is not permitted. If at all there generates any bickering that should be separately discussed.
23. The object of the interrogation must get priority. Any kind of satisfaction, projection, professional realizations etc. may not even be aired in front of the subject.
24. In case of revelation of any interesting point, repeated questioning should be done in order to establish correctness. He may be, if required, questioned about mechanics of collection of the input and the motive behind disclosing the input.
25. Each subjects should be interrogated separately, they may be deprived of consulting each others. But confrontations are allowed to break a subject. Segregation, as far as possible, since the time of arrest, is required primarily to deprive them the opprtunity to consult among themselves.
26. Each subject required to be questioned on each recoveries, their sources and other such details. Details of each address and telephone number recovered must be separately written after ascertaining necessary details from the subject. Pressure be mounted to ascertain the relation/ association with the names of each person figured in these recoveries.

27. Deception, unwillingness and aversion are but natural. Interrogator's mindset, thus, be tough. Creating an urge and impulse in the mind of the subject are much more essential factors. Nervousness of any kind too be removed.
28. High standard of decency, decorum and courtesy should be maintained, specially to women subjects.
29. Specimen handwritings in each language known, photographs, foot and fingerprints, blood samples, voice, etc. of each interrogee should be attached with the I.R.
30. I.R. of each subject must be separately written, as per format.
31. Body language, i.e. verbal and non-verbal communications need to be keenly observed.
32. Rapport building process should start from the entry point.
33. Parting of interrogation, i.e. closing part is also very important.
34. Try to avoid pronouncing threat of punishment. Never utter the penal section and punishment limitations.
35. Hurting of one's religious sentiments often embark to reinforcing dogmatism. Better his religious fanatism may be exploited towards interrogation's end.
36. Privacy is the principal psychological factor, which contribute to the success of interrogation. Distractions, required to be minimized. Thus one should start from non-accusatory to accusatory and the theme may center around to place moral blames on others or the circumstances.
37. Misquotes and answers need proper attention. He may be pursued and provoked till the complete picture is emerged.
38. Bluffing is not advocated in this game, but if at all necessary, well thought of bluffing can be made.
39. Exploiting the ego of the interrogee be made. In spite of apprehension, the subject may suffer from ego problem. Exploitation of his own ego may yield positive result.

40. Face study of the subject be carefully carried out. Face is the index of mind. Face reading, thus, may project true picture and the subject may be grilled upon ascertaining clue from his face reading.

41. Interrogation should be carried according to the code of Laws, Rulings and Instructions and also with regard to age and sex of the subject.

42. Jacob Fisher in his book styled "The Art of Detection" mentions: "The greatest aid, however, will come from investigator's own analysis of each person and situation with which he is confronted. The investigator should realize that every person possesses an affinity, knowledge or attachment for some subject which is close to his heart. Once the investigator invokes the formula by which the door to his subject is opened, full co-operation may generally be secured".

PITFALLS OF INTERROGATION

Interrogation is a game to subjugate a subject with the sharpness of questioning and mesmerizing him through apt handling. It is battle of wits, a psy war. Though there are no laid down or totally accepted norms or techniques recommended for all cases, but there are few time-tested norms and dictums which should be strictly reminded during the course of interrogation. Non-adherence would not only damage the gameplan but could also be counter productive. The don'ts and the compulsorily desired norms are being discussed here.

Team discipline

Interrogations are done by teams. Thus team co-ordination, cohesion, spirit and understanding are must. Any kind of breach or differences is not welcomed. There may be differences in opinion and observation, which should not be aired or projected before the subject. In case of any dispute, the team members may discuss in the adjacent room or in the absence of the interrogee. In-fighting or any kind of bickering among the interrogators are damaging factors and may create unhealthy atmosphere. It is obvious that the credit or discredit shall restore to the team, not upon any individual interrogator.

No direct leading question

During the interrogation, no direct leading question should be put to the interrogee. Obviously, in many cases, the interrogee anxiously awaits for the manner and nature of questionings to gauge knowledge, requirement, depth, etc. of the interrogators. Putting up leading questions shall not only sensitize the subject but also resolute inner strength in him to conceal the just reply. Professional interrogators shower volley of akin or similar typed questions and extract the desired input. The verbal and nonverbal communications are also minutely watched. His body language would produce signs of desperado.

Not to fall prey to cover story

Dodging and out-witting the interrogators are the skills in this game. Thus the cover story bursting at the early stage depends upon the proficiency of any interrogator. The cover story put forward by certain trained and intelligent subject like the Resident Agents, Left Wing Extremist elements, veteran criminals, undercover agents, terrorists are so solid and perfect that only expert and skilled interrogators can burst these covers. These types of subjects in support of consolidation of their covers, often use documents, and even during local verifications their antecedents are also established. Side by side, their revelations too need careful examinations. It is better at the very out-set to listen the cover story forwarded by them and taking cues from their flaws, upon which further grilling may be carried out. More the falsehood, more the chances of faults. The witty and intelligent interrogators rope the subject with the help of his own mistakes. Cover story may also be built soon after arrest. The other kind of criminals/agents are those who live with a permanent cover story. Thus the interrogators should not get swayed with the cover story in any case.

Acting ability

Many clever criminals by way of their acting ability try to outwit the interrogators. Their performance, projection, outbursts, body movement often soften the interrogators. In order to cover their mental feelings, they adopt many syndromes like crying, projecting physical problems, even stop taking food, etc. Trained interrogators know how to counter these concocted behaviours and postures. The interrogators acting ability is a required qualification too.

Do not project any immediate reaction

Projections of any immediate reaction over any interesting or vital revelation made, is not advisable. Barring drawing of the attention of the subject, it may caution the subject who later on try to deny or defy the revelation made. The emotion and body language of the interrogators, create great impact in the mind of the interrogee. One of the required potence of a good interrogator is overall control over his emotion and feelings. Poker faced interrogators, thus, have edge over others.

No hasty conclusion/decision

Drawing of conclusion in haste is also not recommended. During or at the end of any interrogation, team members must sit separately and after discussing pros and cons, they should derive conclusion. One factor is very much significant in this game that there is no scope for majority opinion, even an observation made by a single interrogator might be correct. Therefore, no conclusion may be drawn in haste.

Spoken words can't be retrived

Interrogation is a battle where words are your weapons. Therefore before pronouncement of any word, specially by the interrogators, proper care and caution are needed. Once revealed the said word cannot be retrieved. In case of interrogee the best technique is to defeat and dislodge him by his own utterings.

Don't gossip

Attitudes, handling and desire are the key factors of good interrogators. Their commitment and seriousness in the process create deep impact in the mind of the subject. Gossips would not only disturb the situation but also would tarnish the image of the interrogators. Thus indulgence on gossips should be avoided.

Gossips may change the controlled atmosphere and may off gear the process.

No vague or complex question

The interrogators should not put any vague or complex question. Questions must be brief, pointed, and clearly understood by the subject. If the questions are not properly understood by the subject, how best can he satisfy the team? "Confusing" and "round about" questions are often showered but not the vague ones.

No Biasness

Biasness is a pre-conceived idea. Interrogators must have an open mind and they should be void from any kind of bias or preconceived ideas or opinion. To hate the crime not criminal - must be the motto. Bias often emanates from caste, creed, social status, gender, educational background, political affiliations, religious dogmatism, etc. Professional compulsions too may orient the said feeling. All these are not only derogatory and detrimental towards yielding positive results. These may also squeeze the scope of interrogation. Whereas openmindness accepts and degenerates easy approachability. Apart from bias, the interrogators should not take cognizance of any kind of influence whether it is from within or from outside. All revelations made by the interrogee must be carefully and seriously noted and examined. Many a time, it has been found that the preconceived and prior information proved to be totally incorrect and a complete new picture comes into surface. Interrogators must not incubate incorrect inputs. Professional zeal and interest in upholding the dignity and competency of the concerned department of which they represent, are indispensable requisites, of a good interrogator.

No emotional outburst

One of the basic quality of a good interrogator is control of his emotion and check on his behaviour. He should behave like a normal individual and should not be engrossed with any sort of trait. One of the tact and bearing of interrogation is creating irritation in the minds of the subject. The interrogee may try to irritate the interrogator by keeping silent or by repeating same answers. At no point of time the interrogator should loose control over his emotional outburst. Once the interrogator is emotionally surcharged, his normal feelings, perceptions and reasoning powers got stucked. Many times, the subject adopts a technique to buy the sentiment of the interrogator by telling his woes, which should also be avoided. However, the interrogators must listen, pay proper heed and be sympathetic at times, but they must be devoid of any kind of emotional outburst.

No wooden attitude

In the game of the battle of wits ultimate object is to extract the truth. There must be flexibility in the attitude and everything should be moulded according to situational requirement. Wooden attitude may lead to a wrong conclusion as the subject in order to avoid tortures may agree with the interrogator but in the Court he refutes the revelations made. The best way to extract the truth may be to allow the interrogee to speak and tell his "story" and to take cue from his utterings. He may be confronted on concocted points. When one goes to take any interrogation, he must be enriched with all the necessary information but he must be void of any preconceived idea. Open mindness and free from all kinds of influences are must. During the process of interrogation, gradually one grows his conceptuality and thereby advances towards the desired target. He forms any idea which may or may not be in conformity. Interrogation is a process where anticipation often clicks but from known to unknown and unknown to known areas are also be covered. Flexibilities are must. One should mould according to the circumstances and revelations made. Testing and vetting are also done in order to gauge the truthfulness or otherwise. It is thus safer and wise to bestow the onus on the interrogee and thus grill him taking cue from his revelations. He may be derailed and his deception proceedings may be stucked. He finally will submit himself. Wooden attitude, thus, needs to be avoided and the interrogators should be void from any kind of influences.

Don't take any decision before the subject

Decisions to be taken by the interrogation team, should be taken separately and without the knowledge of the subject. The idea is to keep the subject mentally confused and unstable. He should be in bewilderment. If he is aware of any decision, his mental stress may be lessened and even, in case of anything against him, he would get time to build his defence line. At times, the interrogators may debate among themselves prior to taking any decision, the subject, by listening, would be abreast of both the positive and negative contours, which he may later apply in his defence.

Avoid taking notes before the subject

During the interrogation process, taking notes before the subject is not permitted. The reasons being the subject became conscious and aware of the implication of his revelations. He may spontaneously respond positively to a question but when he visualizes written transformation of his utterings, he becomes extra conscious. Any criminal would try to avoid punishment. Thus taking notes in front of the subject must be avoided. With the advancement of science and technology, bugging and recording devices have become much popular now, even used by private agencies. Where these facilities are not available, one interrogator may be placed in such a location for taking notes, who may invariably be out of sight preview of the interrogee.

Never beg admissions

Never beg admissions to the interrogee, which reflects weakness and incompetence of the interrogators. In interrogation, command and control must be with the interrogators. They should never be allowed to project their weakness or professional lacuna. Begging of admissions might engineer deceptiveness in the minds of the interrogee and he may be more defensive and self-controlled. Interrogation is a psychological game and the interrogator's job is rapport building and then breaking the subject by hook or crook. More emphasis, in case of die-hard subject, may be laid on psychological exploitation, confrontation by pointing both verbal and non-verbal communications of the subject. Interrogators must have upper hand but they must be pragmatic and humane in their attitude. Instead of begging admission, matured interrogators continued their game by putting continuous and "round about" questions and finally extract the relevant input.

No haste please

Interrogation, in criminal investigation, is a key factor. The laws and procedures give a long rope to interrogation gauging importance, gravity and crime sequences. Interrogation is a continuous process. Moreover, interrogation is also a team work. Therefore, there should not be any haste to conclude the interrogation. Interrogation is also not limited to a specific crime. Through interrogation many more information and knowledge on crime world are obtained. In fact, the maxim is, "there is no end to interrogation". A potential interrogee is a treasury of information. Till the total requirements are fulfilled, the process should be on. Even after the official closure of the interrogation a space may be kept opened for future need-based meetings. It should be made systematically, scientifically and in details. However, there are provisions for breaks and rests but the ultimate object is extraction of truth. The continuity of the process shall be determined by the team.

No third degree methods

The term "third degree" is often used to denote physical force used by the police and/or by any security, military and paramilitary forces on a subject mainly to elicit the truth from any suspected or apprehended person. Thus third degree is a very cruel and inhuman method even employed by the interrogators to dig out the truth from a criminal or alike suspects. Paucity of time, lack of adequate training and experience, workload, escalation of terrorist activities, growth of sophisticated and techno crimes, political and public pressure, outcry of media, official pressure are few compulsions which act on the interrogators to adopt easy and quick result oriented method. The fact is this method has been totally banned by the courts. There have been tremendous down fall in adopting this method primarily owing to the verdicts and judgements pronounced by different Courts and for the outcry of the Human Rights and alike bodies. There are pressure to initiate punitive measures against the erring officers. Sec. 29 of the Police Act of 1861 and Art 20(3) of the Constitution of India clearly forbid this inhuman course of action. The interrogator, thus, turns himself as a criminal.

Don't hurt religious sentiments

Religion play an important part in anyone's life, even he may be a criminal. The prime motivation factor of many dreaded terrorist (fundamentalist groups) is religious indoctrination. It is thus not wise to hurt on any interrogee's religious sentiments which might further provoke his religious feelings. However, religion, family affinity and self concerns may be carefully used in bringing back the subject from deceptiveness. Casting venom on one's religion thus be avoided. At times, however, religious books like the Quran, Bible, Guru Granth Sahib, Gita, etc. are placed before in order to psychologically weaken the subject. Displaying of the photographs of the subject's family members are also a technique to woo the sentiments of the subject. If any interrogator starts with paying importance and care of the religiously indoctrinated subject, often he is able to forge rapport at an early stage. Hurting of one's religious sentiment may produce revenge tendencies too.

Don't take revelations on face value

There are a variety of intelligent, veteran and naughty criminals who adopt a technique to avoid prolonged interrogation by revealing and satisfying the interrogator as early as possible. They could assess the requirements of the interrogators through the nature and manners of the questions and stress laid. They do accept a part or so, or even the total crime in such a fashion that he admits the guilt. Thus the interrogators be complaisant and close the interrogation. The golden rule is to testify and verify the revelations made. Detailed interrogation is not only to unearth the crime related inputs for conviction point of view but also generate maximum information from the subject relating crime scenario and even unsolved crimes of similar nature. Accepting a small part of the crime is a generally adopted technique by the veteran and trained subject to avoid torture. Thus he should be grilled for details and there must not be any swathling. Revelations made need proper verification. Knitting of the case from total evidence collection point of view, is also a pointer. Subject's deception capability should be totally crushed.

Cannot be compelled

Proviso of Art 20(3) of the Constitution of India ensures that one cannot be compelled to give evidence against himself save aside an enemy alien or any person who has been arrested or detained under any law providing for preventive detention.

An analysis of the Constitution and other legal provisions reach us to the decision that :

a) An individual is innocent till his guilt is proved.

b) He deserves legal covers and protection.

c) He may not be compelled.

d) He may be non-committal.

e) His arrest needs to be informed to his family members.

f) He is authorized to take legal protection by appointing an Advocate.

g) He may be produced before a magistrate within 24 hours of his arrest.

h) Offence committed by him may be communicated, and

i) He is also covered and protected by certain international laws, statutes and conventions.

Thus during the process of interrogation or prior to it, all these formalities are to be followed and the interrogators should not violate these guidelines. The subject, thus, cannot be compelled to admit his guilt.

Don't allow alcohol and drugs

No drugs or any alcoholic drinks is to be provided to the interrogee. The subject may request for these items but as per rule these items should not be provided. The habitual narcotic drug abuser may even project withdrawal sign. They may better be forwarded to any authorized hospital for treatment. Once ascertained that the subject is a drug abuser, procedurally he should be examined by an authorized physician and the latter's opinion should be taken for further action.

Never interrogate

A seriously injured/critically indisposed subject without the approval of the attending physician. These critically injured subjects, if at all required to be interrogated, presence of and written consent of an authorized medical expert is warranted.

Never make the subject naked

This is a banned technique. But there are sadist natured interrogators found adopting this inhuman technique. The interrogators belonging to the USA have utilized this ghastly and inhuman technique in Iraq and thus earned internationally a very bad reputation. The erring interrogators were booked by the US Courts and they have received punishments for committing the said offence.

PROCESS OR STEPS OF INTERROGATION

Scientific interrogation is never carried out without pre-thinking, adequate preparation made, setting of the objectives and proper briefing. Interrogation per se is quite different from the scientific interrogation of which elaboration are made in the following paragraphs. Interrogation, if we repeat again, is a process available with the investigators to arrive at a conclusion and make prognosis of the subject and the role played by him in the crime context. Invariably it helps in developing the case, culmination and negative directions imbibed around. In modern days sensitive and hard investigation, the role of the experienced and expert interrogators have practically overshadowed other available channels. This type of business never be done without preplanning. In the first place the interrogators should be well abreast of the subject which they are going to cover. Not only the background and antecedents of the interrogee but a solid feedback about his gang/group/organization/party is also to be ascertained. If needed the assistance of the sister organizations, outside states and even of INTERPOL has to be taken. Then comes, proper reference to the available official documents connected with the case. Case referenc, agency who apprehended the subject, circumstances of arrests, recoveries and available intelligence inputs would help in collecting data required to subjugate the subject concerned.

Saying goes, "Winners don't do different things. They do things differently". This saying is absolutely applicable in the context of interrogation. The better the preparation and brain-storming, the perfect the result. Though we may be allowed time space, but finishing up of the task as early as possible be the motto. Delay in breaking the subject is obviously going to provide scope to the co-accused to melt and destroy or conceal the hard evidences. In this techno savvy faster communication age, keeping secret for a longer duration may be a tough job. Moreover, there exists no magical yardstick which can be used to easily subjugate an interrogee and obtain expected result. Goal setting is a-must in this operation and firm determination and conviction are highly needed to elicit favourable responses. Training, knowledge, experience, professional competency and zeal are focused areas. Proper attention, preparation, motivation, procedures, facilities, holistic approach, anticipation, earlier similar case studies, creation of adequate environment, team spirit and drive are also required ingrediences. What all planning and steps be chalked, the interrogee or even those police officers not connected with this task, would be void from knowing.

The following suggestive stages should be systematically followed:

Planning and Preparation

Planning and preparation is a pre-requisite for any type of interrogation. This stage is regarded as the foundation upon which the prognosis of the entire operation shall rely. It is thus the cornerstone. Going through the preliminary interrogation report, if available, case studies, ascertaining the circumstances of apprehension, section of charges levelled, points of suspicion, background checking, inspection of the scene of crime, examinations of the recoveries made, making reference to office records, going through the medical examination report, if appropriately carried out, may be advantageous. The first step starts with the formation of the team or teams. The personality and profile of the subject plays significant role. Whether he has been arrested while commissioning the offence or later on following investigation, acting upon an informer report or alike information, merely on suspicion, on account of his past history, witness, victim, juvenile, lady and foreigners should also be determining factors. This account is likely to provide edge to the interrogators. Scene of crime visit will not only enrich the knowledge and overview but during the process of interrogation, the interrogators would be able to connect the revelations made and even be in a better position to put cross questions. Ascertaining the modus operandi i.e. style of working or mode of operation, would naturally be advantageous for the interrogators to advance the case and corner the interrogee. Modus operandi is likely to be a distinctive feature. Clever criminals may change or make alteration to give dodge to the interrogators.

At this stage, problem may arise to access about a new-comer or even a member of an organization background of which is not available in the office. In the later case a reference may be made to the concerned State or Central Government for providing necessary feedback. Assistance of the sister agencies like the Intelligence Bureau, Subsidiary Intelligence Bureau, Research and Analysis Wing, SSB, DRI, NCB, BSF and other such bodies may also be solicited in formulating a comprehensive idea about the subject and also his organization. Reference may also be made to the Crime Record Bureau of both the State as well as the Center. At this stage the objective of the case, team formation, selection of a team leader, setting up of a Control Room, arrangements of the Interrogation Room, requisition for technical gadgets, logistics like transport, communication facilities, and other necessary backups are also to be determined.

This stage is reckoned to be very vital and thus every tits and bits are to be discussed, planned and if necessary their operational capabilities are to be checked. There are cases where the particular subject was subjected to interrogation earlier, specially in the cases of veteran criminals, underground operators, terrorists, militants, drug peddlers, smugglers, touts etc., their earlier IR may also be consulted to obtain a complete picture about the subject and also about his criminal nexus. In some significant cases, the CID or Special Branch may also be consulted for obtaining feedback from them. It must be checked whether the interrogee is in Police or Jail remand and for how many days.

Planning schedule will be done accordingly. In few cases it is prudent if discreet local enquiries are conducted about the interrogee to ascertain his strong and weak points, family background and even nationality. The state of health of the interrogee is a key concern. In the event of a complete new and typical case, mirror imaging technique, in consultations, remains the only way out.

Considered view and more focus are warranted while interrogating or interviewing a victim. The victim, in criminology, has earned wide ramifications as the same natured offences have clubbed together. As for example, while we take the case of a particular rape victim for consideration, a pressure is naturally mounted owing to wide coverage of the word "rape". The sympathy for the victim is also likely to add new dimension. Similar with the case of juvenile offenders as well of victims. There are certain crimes which generate society or natural's attention and thus the interrogators suffer from pressure too. The outcry and publicity also mount pressure. Planning and determination thus matter much. It may be kept in mind that the outcome of any interrogation is going to have much impact over the case and also on the subject. Very judicial and perfect view is also required. Interrogators process thus should not be too vindictive or harsh. Pragmatic and effective attitude should promote the process. Contributory negligence on the part of the interrogating team members cannot be supported. Punitive vengeance on the wrong doer exists but retaliatory actions are never supported. The interrogation should also be non-distinctive on counts of race, sex, age, language, caste, religion, nationality, culture, political leanings, status and belief. Interrogators should resolute be free from any conviction, pre-conceived idea, influence, prejudice and ill-feelings. Law abidingness, reverence to the ethics, respect to the organization's goodwill and due regard to the profession are code of conducts which the interrogators must adhere to.

Team Formation

Interrogation is considered as a costly affairs on account of involvement of many trained and experienced officers for a prolonged period. It is carried out not by an individual but by teams. Each team is constituted by at least three to four trained interrogators. Teams do rotate as per demand of the case. The timings are also adjusted as per requirements. Prolonged continuity of interrogation has been viewed as promulgation of third degree or mental torture. Few analysts viewed that an intensive interrogation amounts to torture where the subject is deprived of rest and respite. While pronouncing judgement in Amrut v. State of Bombay [AIR 1960 Bombay 488] the court held that where the statements leading to the discovery of things were made to the police as a result of harassment and continuous interrogation for several hours after a person is treated as an accused, such statements must be discovered as involuntary and as such hit Art 20(3) of the Constitution of India which guarantees freedom against testimony compulsion. In the light of the above judgement and other such verdicts pronounced by the Apex Court, it is necessary not to deny food, drinking water, toileting facilities, sleep and other civic facilities to the subjects.

Each team should have a leader and a team coordinator. These should be prefixed. In interrogation there is no rank consciousness. Experience, ability, knowledge about the tradecraft, are the yardsticks of evaluation. Normally one leader is selected, in advance, to supervise, coordinate and guide the interrogators. He is the link between the process and the office too. After selection of the team members, briefings are made, team cohesiveness, unison and understanding are necessary to emanate an effective result. The team members should avoid individualistic approach and self-estimation. It is the bounden duty of each interrogator to pre-determine the type of role he is going to play during this process. Any difference of opinion or confusion, the interrogators should refrain from openly discussing it in presence of the subject. They may also not quarrel among themselves. The differences need to be amicably settled. Team spirit pose deterrent effect on the subject. Interrogators further be apprised about the credit or discredit, as it would be shared among the team members and not by any specific interrogator.

Interrogation Room Preparation

Environment plays a significant effect in the interrogation process. Recommended theory is systematic and unabated process. Therefore, in the planning and preparation stage much attention should be paid not only on the selection of the place but also for arranging necessary requirements. In normal cases a room in the police station itself is converted to an interrogation room. Interrogation is not to be carried out at the residence of the interrogee barring the cases of a few victims. Interrogation is also debarred at the residence of a police officer for security and safety reason. The place selected should be a safe, secured and secluded one. Necessary facilities should also be there.

Briefing and Preparation of Probable Questionnaires

The outcome of any interrogation is extremely dependent on briefing made and well chalking of probable questionnaires. Briefing is defined as a process of imparting instructions by the controlling officer regarding ways and means to complete the assigned task. It has, therefore, direct bearing on result orientation. It provides and covers all the necessary aspects including a tradecraft knowledge i.e. do's and don'ts, pitfalls methodologies or techniques to be adopted, and the overall assessment of the case as well as of the subject concerned. The hazards, risks, problems, constraints and the likely hindrances are also anticipated and discussed. Knowledge and experience sharing are also inherent in it. Tasking means the assigned job while briefing provides direction and elaborate knowledge about procedures to accomplice the task. Thus briefing covers wide dimension. Prior to imparting briefing indepth studies about the concerned case, the subject and the purpose of the interrogation should deeply be carried out. Briefing is always done in a congenial atmosphere, in clear and well understood language, point wise, covering both positive and negative points and restricted to the assignment only. It is wise to evaluate whether the briefing made has been properly consumed or not. During the course of briefing if any suggestion, problem or likely difficulty or even any personal problem is raised by any interrogator, that should be carefully taken into account and if necessary, decision for redressing may be taken. Briefing should also be void from any confusion and motivation aspect may also be kept in view. Demotivating factors, if any, should also be removed. Briefing includes training part too. Neo-crimes and neo-modus operandi, if any engrossed in the case, should invariably be discussed. Secrecy of the briefings need to be kept and the principle of restrictive security should also be adhered to. Briefing not only generate clarity and gravity of the assigned tasking i.e., the interrogation per se, but also enrich the working spree of the interrogators as well as help in forging team spirit and discipline.

As already explained, interrogation is the art of questioning. The entire process is governed and controlled by dialogues how best you can put and extract information. Questioning i.e., the weightage, sharpness, mode, manner and meaning, do act upon the inner surface of the interrogee. In interrogation, the interrogators are not supposed to put any direct question to the subject on count of providing scope to the later about understanding the intention and purpose of the interrogation. Therefore, a lot of brain storming process is required to be activated prior to selecting any question hence, the probable questions. Secondly, it shall help the interrogators to check whether any vital question has been omitted or not. The team prepares the list in consultation, and the team leaders should approve it. While preparing this list, attention and focus should be paid on sequence and weightage. Never put any hard or complicated question at the initial stage. Crime connected questions too need to be avoided prior to breaking up of the subject.

Questions may be of several types and dimensions. Namely :

1. *Relevant :* Relevant i.e. essentially needed for developing the case and collecting evidences of value.
2. *Irrelevant :* i.e. not connected with the concerned case. These questions are put to distract the stiff and rigid attention of the subject and soften him to speak. This process is nothing but to break silence of the interrogee.

3. *Opened :* Where the subject has to go in for elaboration. He won't be able to control his revelations in a word or two. Opened questions also provide wide scope of generation of sub-questions. Thus this type of question is always preferable.

4. *Closed :* It means and includes a question where the reply may be limited by way of pronouncing "yes" or "no", "don't know" type of reply. These questions are not encouraging and be, thus, avoided. The subject gets lot of respite in answering these questions.

5. *Direct bearing :* The questions which form essential component and the body of the case. There are, thus, differences between "relevant" and "direct bearing" questions. Relevant questions are associated with the case while "direct bearing" questions are essential component of the case, bearing prosecutive value.

6. *Rapport building :* The questions, mainly motivating, gaining sympathy, enlarging apathy, projecting personal concern are essential part of rapport building. These are soft, polite in language and coined in such a nature which can create impulse in one's mind. These are put very carefully after evaluating the gross total of the case.

7. *Controlled :* Well balanced questions having high edge. The meaning of these questions can also be moulded.

8. *Irritating or Provocating :* These natured questions are levelled to irritate the subject and thereby to decontrol his deceptiveness. Questions should create an urge in the mind of the subject to speak. Therefore, the irritating or provocating questions are put to destabilize one's overt control. He became infuriated in such a way that his reasoning power is lost. In the fit of rage or irritation, the subject is likely to come out with the truth.

9. *Compassion :* Compassion bounded questions provide mental solace as well as keep the subject away from the crime scenario for the moment. Human nature is besieged with gratification and also flattery. Compassion is little away

i.e. to get close to the heart. The subject finds someone sympathetic.

10. *Informative :* Data collection is one of the objectives of interrogation. Through it lot of information is generated. Informative questions are those which are aimed to garner information of interest from a potential subject.

11. *Short end :* Short question is viable as it limits the variation of the reply. It is much fruitful in the mid-session where exact replies are needed.

12. *Long end :* Long end provides vast scope to explain and elaborate the facts and inputs. The cleaver interrogators allow the subject to speak broadly and from his uttering clues are derived for further questioning.

13. *Follow up :* Follow up questions are those which are projected to go further into the deep. Obtaining of details is the purpose.

14. *Assumptive :* Anticipation is a beauty in itself. The experience and knowledge of the interrogators are of paramount importance in this game. Hence, the scope of assumptive or presumptive questions.

15. *Indirect :* Majority questions, during the process, are indirect in nature. How you are going to twist the question, is the art.

16. *Round about :* Round about questions are put ostensibly to filter the truth. if we put any question having direct bearing, is likely to arise consciousness in the mind of the subject. If the questions are having no direct touch but are aimed with the idea to hit the bull, the purpose may be fulfilled. Involvement of the subject, inspection of the scene of crime, examination of the recoveries and revelations made by co-accused are vital components of the source of round about questions.

17. *Repeated :* Questions are repeated to confirm the revelations and also to make these more distinctive. Repeated replies shall be a process of correcting errors, if any.

18. *Testing* : Few intelligent and well formulated questions are made for testing the subject. Testing questions should be forwarded prior to taking final decision over any revelations.
19. *Checking* : Checking and vetting are recommended theories to be followed. Checking of the prior revelations should be done, if possible after a plausible gap. Let the subject repeat his earlier version. Discrepancies may be noted and again re-checking may be conducted.

Detailed discussions about questioning have been made in a separate chapter. However, questionings require planning, intelligent mind, sharpness, presence of mind and experience. When and how to put a question, the timing is adjusted and adjudicated by the interrogators.

Medical examination of the subject

Subject's condition of health has got direct bearing on interrogation. Unwell or ill subject would not be able to concentrate. Though interrogation is a formal process of criminal investigation, yet the generation and extraction of the concealed part of information, is the goal. Medical examination, soon after the arrest, is imbibed in the procedure. In the planning and preparation stage, conduction of further medical examination of the interrogee, is also chalked out. The main purpose remains orbited around ascertaining the exact state of health condition of the interrogee, being prescribed by an authorized medical practitioner. If he is recommended as "fit to undergo interrogation", then only the process should start. This procedure shall also provide protection to the interrogators. Any adverse health condition or even the death of the interrogee during the course of interrogation, shall rope the interrogators and make them liable for punitive action too. There are evidences where the detained subject was subjected to torture while in the lock up and the interrogators were quite unaware of these actions. Therefore, before taking to custody for interrogation, formal medical examination of the interrogee is suggested.

Clever and veteran criminals often take plea of their illness. It is thus preemptive to get clearance from the competent physician. During the course of interrogation, the subject may express physical problems which too be attended and examined. In case of any serious natured problem, it is wise to refer him to nearby medical unit. However, deceptiveness in this respect should not be encouraged. Never try to treat any interrogee on your own. The subject may suffer from various health hazards.

Moreover, the arrest may give rise to sugar, blood pressure, heart related problems besides mental agony and bewilderness. The totality may only be prognosised by the competent physician. Another point which is required to be given weightage is to interview a subject in the hospital or in any medical unit where he is undergoing treatment. In this case, physician's permission may be accorded and he should be interviewed in the presence of a doctor.

Frisking and Search

It is important to carry out body search of the interrogee prior to the initiation of interrogation. It is nothing but a precautionary measure to detect presence of any incriminating object which, if used by the interrogee, may be fatal. A thorough search not only of the person, but also of his belongings, room and even the surrounding areas are procedural in presence of independent witness. As per proviso of the Cr PC women are to be searched by lady only. A seizure list, enlisting every details, is also prepared following the codes and procedures.

Marks of injuries, scars, bullet injury marks, marks on palms or fingers, tattoo marks and physical deformities are positive and noticeable points of markings. Questions may be raised to ascertain details of these markings from the interrogee. Only plausible answers should be taken into consideration. The subject is required to be grilled to speak the truth and not any concocted version. These marks may not be noticed by initial searchers. These require minute observation too. These are, however, pointers to many undisclosed facts which may not even be anticipated. The tailor marks, washerman's marks of the wearing of the subject should also be examined. Searches are mainly carried out to detect any extraneous items supplied to him even after the arrest. Any suspected or incriminating item found, needs proper examination including its origin.

Any new item found should invariably be incorporated in the concerned Seizure List and be brought to the notice of the IO. This procedure, prior to taking up any interrogation, is nothing but a precautionary measure adopted by the interrogating team members to avoid any mishap.

Pick up or Initiation

Picking up i.e. entry behaviour is also a significant part. There is a saying that love at first sight or first impression is the last impression. In fact the subject remains in a mentally surchaged position as many odds travel through his mind. His anticipated idea and conception regarding the interrogators make him more confused. He eagerly awaits for personal view of the interrogations and also tries to access the nature, personality and other behavioural attitudes linked with the interrogation. The entry behaviour i.e. the dress, physical feature, voice, personality and the initial sentences are not only minutely observed by the interrogee but also create an impact in his mind. Thus it is considered as a crucial part. There are no prescribed or standard specification in this respect. It shall entirely be chalked out by the interrogators considering the status, standard, experience, crime in which he is involved, education, social status, age, sex and family condition of the subject. It is, however, better to first start with non-formal areas. Crime and punishment portions never be referred at the beginning. Asking of welfare, physical condition, discomfort, lock up conditions, food, sleep and even enquiring about establishment of contacts with family members shall provide a solace to him. He will find someone at least concerned for him. These polite, soft and touchy non-formal interactions may also help in buying the sympathy of the subject. Never start with bully or filthy natured attacking dialogues which not only infuriat the psyche of the subject but also engineer a "hate relationship" with that particular interrogator. He shall, thereby, try to distance himself away from that very interrogator. Profession and hobbies are other likely common topics which may be a good starter. Never treat a subject as weak nor innocent at the outset. Thumping of command and control do not mean underestimating any interrogee. Creation of fear psychosis in the mind of the subject and stepping up of pressure be there. Respect is something but never offer "Sir" etc. Let him feel that he is an interrogee and devoid from officialdom or whatsoever status. Treat him as a common man. Avoid putting any serious natured question at the initial stage. It may further act on his disturbed mind and he may loose mental tranquility and equilibrium. A good professional always tries to cheer up, bring him to normal condition and gradually rope him. Avoid to be much sympathetic or concern about him, he may capitalize these as interrogator's weakness and further put pressure towards solving his problems or difficulties. Better an equidistance should be maintained. Purpose of the interrogation should be the guiding principle. There are, however, controversies whether shaking of hand with the interrogee is permissible or not. Majority experts are holding negative opinion in this respect. Let develop some command ground to initiate conservation. Creation of "urge to speak" be the motto.

Sizing Up

In many cases, paper studies may not help in creating an overall view about the subject. An interrogator only activate his line of thinking after the perusal of the subject. Sizing up means and includes profiling the interrogee in the correct perspectives. Unluckily there is no measurement or evaluatory gauge, only by way of tactful and purposeful conversations proper lining up of the subject is possible. The PART - I of the IR is, thus, stated to be the pivotal lines, which should be minutely, systematically and seriously drawn. It is rather a brief bio-data of the subject reflecting his family, education, profession, financial condition, linkages, status and other personal data. Emergence of these strong and weak points shall provide enough and wide scope to have an estimation of the subject whom the interrogators are likely to deal with. The potentiality of the subject as well as his "soft" areas could also be gauged and clues for twisting or moulding the subject may be obtained from these points. Sizing up and rapport building may run simultaneously. Once the proper estimation is done, tackling becomes easier. A competent interrogator always pays much heed in this aspect. He could smoothly sail the business. Sizing up of the interrogee not only is aimed to narrowing the focused area but also good pointer to outwit the strong presence of resistance in him. Once proper profiling is done, the technicalities of the operation become easier. Human factor, as explained earlier, should be the governing principle.

Rapport Building

A very hard and trust area in the process. Establishing a rapport means building up of a harmonious relationship, to forge an understanding and winning the heart of the interrogee. The faster and quicker the rapport building process, the better and formidable the outcome. It is indeed a deep, emotional and psychological approach between two different persons. The concern, touch, sympathy, courteous attitude, sentimental conversation, emotional appeal, affinity, smiles, openness and relaxed and friendly atmosphere obviously mould the subject and create an impulsive impact in his mind. These would initiate a feeling of reciprocity as well help in removing fear from his mind. Relaxed conversations, softer words, not offering any blasting question, projection of emotion are also few desired norms. It is suggested that topics of mutual interests, common ground, explaining benefits of co-operation are also few areas which govern the scope and utility of this process. Looking after the material needs of the subject and allowing him to identify himself are other aspects of concern.

Individualistic approach and activating of the cultural, religious, family, educational, social and status scopes of the interrogee may awaken his good senses and may help in rapport building. It is better to give him a long rope. Detection of his feelings, anxiety, frustration, conflicts, anger and other mental and emotional outbursts would also help in the rapport building process. Each individual inherits some likes and dislikes as well some subject close to his heart. Therefore, the need to properly sizing up of the psychological treatment to the extent needed. Intellectual level of the subject too matters much. Personality and ego problems are also reckoning factors. Continuous and serious efforts should be made till culmination of the success. No analysis can be regarded as successful without retrieval of sufficient reliable information. The tact, talent and experience of the interrogators may also be gauged from the success record of this process.

Breaking Up

The core object of the entire interrogation is bestowed on co-operation and willingness of the subject to reveal the truth. Deception is a normal and quite expected attitude. Everyone, initially, shall put his endeavour to prove himself innocent. Thus falsehood, lies, fabrication are but natural. Hard and controlled effects of the interrogators, after all put mental pressure on the subject and prepare him to reveal the truth. It is known as breaking up of the interrogee. Now he is ready to answer on the right direction. The role of apt questioning now dominates the scene. Prudency of an interrogator is judged weighting the mode, manner and form of the questions. Subject may provide a partial reply, knowingly or unwillingly. Extraction of the full text is the beauty. The point of agreement and dis-agreement may be there. Vetting is to be done. Much precautions and threadbear analysis should be done prior to taking any decision. Once the interrogee has started sharing, blackmailing can be done in case of his intermittent non-cooperation. Dealing and handling of the interrogee shall form effective part of this business. Never allow the subject to ascertain your points of interest. Be casual but firm.

Confrontation

Confrontation is the face to face ordeal and arguments. It is a usual technique adopted to force him to reveal the truth. Confrontation may be made with the revealed matter of the co-accused, face to face dialogues or even by producing recoveries. Verbal and non-verbal communications and recorded pictures should also be the matter. At times, when prior to apprehension, clandestine photography or videography is done, these may also be the confrontation objects. The interrogees are also confronted with the clandestinely recorded telephonic conversations. Confrontations, thus, is also an intelligent format in the process.

Popularly weakest of any team (when more than one is arrested in the same case) is taken for interrogation and his revelations after evaluation, is used as confrontation matter. In case of anyone's tough posture, the said weakest team member is confronted face to face with the tough one. The latter becomes deprived to gain any respite owing to the discloser made by a team member. When confrontation is made vice other items as mentioned above, the interrogee should be allowed to role out. He will not be able to suppress the truth for longer duration.

Evaluation

Revelations made are not the goal of any interrogation. Extraction of truth and the "concealed part" are the core components. Interrogee is likely to speak, even a volume. He being a criminal, is habituated of deceptive tendencies. Trained and religiously indoctrinated criminals are more serious in this matter. Thus, the revelations made should be vetted, corroborated and if necessary may be enquired into. The logic is to examine the veracity of the statements. Office records checking, scene of crime visit, examinations of the recoveries, examining the witness, local verifications, secret enquiries conducted through the sources and contacts, are few avenues available with the investigators to verify any uttering. In case of any reference made pertaining to other jurisdiction or even out of state, the concerned authorities may also be consulted. Time factor, i.e. the speed of these verifications must be maintained. While probing or conducting any enquiry, secrecy should be maintained. Otherwise the very purpose of the enquiry may be defeated. There are many instances when openly conducted enquiry enabled the group members/ co-accused to go underground and few of them could leave India forever. However, the correctness of the statement made, must be authentic and void from any ill design. The time span remains so limited that a formation of a separate team becomes necessary to probe the revelations made by the interrogee. It is suggested that modern faster communication channels be used and telephone request may be made to the other ends for the feedback to save time consumption.

Parting Up

Parting up is the closer of the process. It is bidding farewell from the interrogee. It is also viewed as a reminding factor as you are leaving your last impression. Creation of enemies is not the purpose of interrogation. Through this process a good interrogator establishes a bond of understanding, trust and friendship with the interrogee. Cultivation of contacts and sources are also possible by following the intelligence tradecraft norms. In our criminal justice system it is difficult to keep a criminal in jail for a longer duration barring awarding capital punishment. The subject is likely to return to his society and many a time again join the gang/group/organization he belonged. Through him the coverage of these areas and generation of operational intelligence are possible. Good behaviour, soft handling, sympathy and mind-boggling are the ways and means through which cultivation could be possible. Negatively hurting and humiliating the subject tantamount to creation of an enemy.

Comments

In interrogation there remains very little scope to reflect the opinions of the interrogators. The IR is the written elaboration of the verbatim revelations made by the interrogee. At points, there may be differences of opinions among the team members. That's why the provision for "comment" column in the IR, wherein the interrogators observation, suggestion, interpretation and remark are noted for the perusal of the controlling officer. This part is separately written and pinned with the same report. It may, if necessary, be detached from the main IR for operational use. In fact many IRs reflect "inputs" of interest which are separately developed. One must be judicious, clear and void from any prejudices while writing this part. As far as possible negative aspects may be avoided as these would obviously go against efficiency of the interrogators. Only important and significant points may be reflected.

QUALITIES OF A GOOD INTERROGATOR

Dr. Hans Gross, an eminent authority on criminal investigation, observed that it goes without saying that an investigator should be endowed with all those qualities which every man should desire to possess — indefatiagable zeal and application, self-denial and perseverance, swiftness in reading men and a thorough knowledge of human nature, education and encyclopedic knowledge. These virtues are required to be cultivated, inculcated and also are to be necessarily displayed while on job by the interrogators. Trainings can mould, increase and enhance knowledge, skill and attitude but in interrogation, the practice sharpens the edge. Tradecraft knowledge and know-how are matters of complements. Basically the wisdom, determination, anticipation, aspiration, professional acumenship, curiosity, interest and thrive are also formidable components which an able and apt interrogator should own. These qualifications and other such faculties are the pre-requisites of a good interrogator. Interrogation is regarded as a battle of wits and psy-war where the winning scale is the knowledge, skill, wisdom and situational advantage. Human instincts and factors do prevail. In this battle both the interrogator and the interrogee vie to win and to outwit the opponent by talent, tact and trial. Interrogees are used to play mostly a defensive game, while the proven interrogator always purposefully dislodge the defence strategies as well as the deception endeavour. Misbalancing and disbanding mental consolidation and tranquility of the subject are the expected dubbings of this game. Bringing back to normalcy and roping up of the subject in order to force him to subjugate are always a tough job. Nonetheless it is a psy-war i.e. a psychological confrontation or tussle where all the players are rational animals. Interestingly both the fronts, in a democratic set up like ours, are well guarded and protected by legal covers. There are also many checks and bounds. Interrogees should never be viewed as weak, un-intelligent and less professionals. Negatively the subjects connected with counter-intelligence, terrorist, militants and even underground fields of operation might have enriched knowledge and conviction. Their countering and dodging capabilities might also be superior and well fabricated. Therefore the quality and qualification of the interrogators count much in their drive to win the battle. Personality, confidence, determination, command and control play pivotal role in this crucial confrontation. Mind reading i.e. psychological analysis of the prevailing state of mind of the subject not only helps in handling the situation but also further the case towards achieving the success. It may, however, be aptly done. Jacob Fisher in his book "The Art of Detection" (1948/ New Brunswick/USA) observed, "The good investigator must be a practical psychologist and a study of this subject may help in the handling of the people. The greatest aid, however, will come from investigator's own analysis of each person and situation with which he is confronted. The investigator should realize that every person possesses an affinity, knowledge or attachment for some subject which is close to his heart. Once the investigator invokes the formula by which the door to his subject is opened, full cooperation may generally be secured." The best method in ascertaining the psychological impact, is to put oneself in the position of the other i.e. the interrogator should understand the cause and effect alighting in the mind of the subject. The interrogator should obviously advance in a very cautious way. Subject's conduct, demeanour, verbal and non-verbal communications need to be minutely observed. Seriousness is the most wanted dogma in this process. The best noticeable part of any interrogation is his approachability, temper and disciplined behaviour. Creation of a congenial and comfortable atmosphere besides stimulating the subject i.e. creating an urge, are also necessary elements. Interrogators having analytical mind and systematic attitude prove to be more effective in this game. The way of handling the situation and the covert seriousness displayed are other significant complements.

A good interrogator must inculcate the quality to dominate the scene and his leadership ability. It counts much. By virtue of his commanding authority, he should prevail upon the subject and also to ride over the negative overtures projected by the latter. The interrogee should feel that he is in conversation with a reliable and dependable officer who is concerned about his problems, standings and view points. A professional interrogator seldom sneers, ridicules, bullies, belittles, antagonizes, loses his temper, makes false promises, project casualness and ill-treats the subject. He is always a patient listener, a mentor and a balanced reformer. The role played and the acting ability too, throughout the process, are other highlights. Mannerism, respect and adherence towards the rule of law and code of conducts, respect towards own's religion, caste and sex are few added overtures which not only help in rapport building endeavour but also are reckoned as microscopic advantages. Distasteful talks, idiotic behaviour, bad mannerism and postures are graded as negative counts. Therefore, it is said that the prognosis of any interrogation rests upon the potency and quality of the interrogators. Few qualities may be in-born and a few may be cultivated. The interrogators are, therefore, the driving force and their actions, dealings and knowledge count much in this process of investigation. Let us now discuss, in brief, few most sought after qualities which the interrogators should possess :

Encylopaedic Knowledge

Knowledge is wisdom. Knowledge is power. It is the forearm of an interrogator. Knowledge should be all rounded, not specific to criminal science only. The scope of general knowledge is much indicative. It should be in such a pitch, which could easily be retrieved and connected. Knowledge about the topography, locality, pockets of influence, targets, ideologies, dogmas, composition, leadership, command structure, training, motivation, psychology and human behaviour would provide edge in this process of criminal investigation. Detailed knowledge and perception on technical and electronic operations and knowhow are other aspects of interest. Interrogators, thus, be ready reckoner type and their knowledge treasury would be meaningful in this process.

Personality

Personality dignifies an individual and a class in itself. It is the quality which prevails upon and acts upon the interviewer/ interrogee. It is the most visible conceptualization of a person's behaviour, in all its details, and is subjected to change or may be adjusted as per situational need.

Dress Code

There exists no recommended dress code for the interrogators. Uniformed police, however, don their prescribed uniform.

Favourable responses and impacts may be generated in civilian clothes. Police uniform might promote nervousness and fear-psychosis in the minds of the weak interrogees, nervous witness, children and few victims. Uniform not only signifies the position of the interrogator but also exposes his name and designation. It further helps in creating a barrier between the interrogee and the interrogator, produces psychological impulses, consciousness and defensive attitude. Uniform has got deterrent standing, specifically a damaging factor in rapport building as the criminals per se do harbour allergies and antipathies towards the police and intelligence officials. According to them, police reckoned to be the instrument to inflinch punishment and rarely could be trusted upon. On the contrary civilian orientation of an interrogator provides ample elasticity and flexibility and at times the subject's mind may be erased that he is under interrogation. Civil clothes further provide acting scope and the interrogator can fit himself in the befitting role. He can also demonstrate himself freely and effectively. He is able to focus as per his will and without any hindrances, prejudices or constraint. Each uniform has got certain codes which are required to be maintained and followed. It is rather tough to relax by donning uniform. Revolver or pistol forms a part of uniform too. The subject's attention obviously be drawn and an adverse or panicky impact is likely to emerge. It may create repulsive effect too.

An interesting judgement pronounced by the Judiciary in DK Basu vs. State of W.B. (AIR 1997 S C 610) which inter alia mentioned that while interrogating a person the police officers should bear accurate, visible and clear identification and name tags with their designation. In other way, the subject would be able to know who are the police officers interrogating him. A record in this regard is also to be maintained. Intelligence wing personnel do not customarily wear any uniform. This measure provides them good cover too. Officials of the intelligence wings and organizations, owing to their expertise, are often deployed in interrogating hard and prized subjects. Civilian dress should be such that signify and denote personality of the interrogator. It should be simple, comfortable and not gorgeous. It must make a sense. It may also be adjusted with the climatic condition as well, cleanliness should also be paid on shoes, hair cuttings and shaving. Vulgar dress, and erotic costumes are not permitted. Experts differ on wearing pure casual wears including chappal. A group is of the opinion that jean, T-shirt, chappal are good cover to hide one's police identity. Others do not sanction such casuals, rather view that dress should command personality. Whatever might be, proper selection and adjustment do matter in order to create confidence, forge friendship and derive respect. Shabby, dirty and gorgeous dress invariably would produce negative impact.

Education and Training

Education means and includes both the formal and informal education of the interrogator. In fact the dearth of educational background, knowledge relating to socio-economic conditions, administrative steps, local laws and other institutions, religious feelings, habits, social norms, human physiology and psychology, behavioural sciences, social problems, family fabric, on-going criminal scenario, prevailing law and general knowledge have direct or indirect bearings in this process. Education further emboldens judiciousness. It emanates perfection and promotes confidence. It helps in goal-fixing and finally eliminates the barriers. Professional competency of any interrogator is adjudicated vying on his speed and adjustability in the job. One of the criteria fixed while selecting an interrogator is that he should be trained in interrogation tradecraft. Training not only moulds an officer but also professionalizes him so as to undertake the assignment competently and confidently. Objective of any training per se is three folds, namely upgrading of the knowledge, skill and attitude. One of the benefits of training is inculcation of knowledge about neo-techniques, introduction of new technological and electronic gadgets. Interrogators must, therefore, be trained in this specialized art. In this field too, day by day modus operandi and techniques go on changing rapidly. Therefore, both the education and the trainings of the interrogators are matters of significance concern.

Intelligence

Intelligence as interpreted is a mode or way of acting in a situation. It has, therefore, got a direct bearing on interrogation, particularly the intelligence of any interrogator is a cognitive factor with reference to higher thought process. Cognitive faculties like observation or imagination, conception, reasoning and determination are also included within the meaning of intelligence. Though the term intelligence is a noun in form, in interrogation it is also used as a verb or adverb form. It also denotes the capacity for solving the problems. It is indicated by the ability to successfully deal with novel situations or quickly avoid such ones as are unsuccessful. Interrogators and occupational adjustments should run together to achieve maximum success rate in this process. In the making and gauging of professional competency and brilliancy of any interrogator, count or scaling of intelligence have got substantial value.

Experience

One of the required qualities of any interrogation is that the interrogators be experienced. Experience includes both observation and experiment. Some forms of experience include sensation, perception, memory, imagination which are major component involved in the process of interrogation. Criminology regards experience as the foremost quality of any investigator. Critical and analytical estimations of interrogees are serious passing points, derive much attention production of variable results and introspection also depend upon the experience of the performers, in this case, the interrogators. Experience of the interrogators is regarded as the thought process and provocateur in the motivation, penetration and punctuated in the inner circle of the interviewer. Thus, experience is another required aspect of a good interrogator. Without experience it may be difficult on the part of the interrogator to tackle and deal with the veteran, die-hard and committed criminals.

Good Motivator

A good interrogator should also be a potential motivator. His ability and proficiency to subjugate the interrogee is a matter of extreme interest. To motivate means to energise or incite or enforce activity. In other words, it means to supply the spring or source of action. Drive, need, motive and incentive are few forces which constitute motivation. It is an activation from within the organism. It may be done by both consciously or unconsciously. The end-term of the process of motivation is the state of fulfillment of the need. In interrogation the need is to "break the subject" and extraction of the truth. The very quality of a good interrogator, therefore, centred around motivating the subject and removal of all existing odd conceptions and conditions prevailing in the mind's of the interrogee. Thus each interrogator should inculcate the required impulses to create an urge to be truthful. Knowledge of human psychology is also an essential requirement. Creation of required stimulus and keen observation and analytical study of the subject are the guiding principles underlined in this process of investigation. Interrogators while playing the role of motivators, should also equally think of "social motive" while interviewing victims of the rape cases, children and alike witnesses. Ego, social prestige and power, high ambitious people and conscious criminals do deserve special attention while displacement, bewilderment, aloneness, blackmailing, regression are few advantageous points. Thus the prudence of the interrogator may be estimated with the ability of motivation capability.

Knowledge about Technical Gadgets

Interrogation is no more limited to human resources only. We have discussed, in a separate chapter about the use of few scientific equipments in unearthing truth from the interrogees. These gadgets and few tested methodologies are now in random use. Therefore the interrogators should be well abreast of and acquainted with these gadgets, their utilities and proper handling, if required. Majority of these equipments are handled by the recognized experts but it is the interrogators who briefs and often directs these experts about the case vis-à-vis the subject's probable leanings. With the gradual development of science and technology, updated knowledge on this score is much sought after for. The thrust for perfection and strong will for proper result orientation on the part of the interrogators are acknowledged areas of attention. They should know the plus and minus points of these evolved technologies in use.

Will

Will or determination is the highest conative process which emboldens an interrogator in his conscious effort in fulfilling the objectives incorporated in any interrogation. Responsibility and obligation are among the determining factors to form a strong will. Good intention too promotes solid will. Strong motivation, feeling of need, desire, benefit, satisfaction, individual image, reputation earning and character help in building positive will even in the mind of the interrogators. Will is also termed as "focus" in interrogation. It is obviously a mental phenomenon but in interrogation it is distinctively connected with the promotion of result. Strong will negates all the conflicts too and overcomes resistances. Interrogators without any determination may be swayed away by the deceptive subjects. Therefore, the phenomenon.

Good Reflex

Alertness and good reflex actions are also qualities which should accomplice a good interrogator. Sharpness and ability to cue any point limited by the subject are precisely the product of reflex actions. A reflex is a non-voluntary action produced by an inter-organic or extra-organic stimulus following upon its representation immediately, simply and uniformly. Those interrogators who are having good reflexes, are proved to be much successful in interrogation.

Sharp Attention

Uncareful mind and casualness are the negative qualities while interrogator having sharp attention are veined more potent one. Attention is that general mental activity which narrow down the field of consciousness to the focus by withdrawing the mind from irrelevant object in the margin. Attention focuses consciousness upon a single object forcing irrelevant objects to the background and makes the object clearly and distinctly known. It is the feature of concentration on the subject and therefore it helps in result orientation. It includes a complex of sensation and idea and also the act of concentrating the mind upon the subject. Therefore the interrogators with brilliance focus the attention and could easily prevail upon the subject. It adds distinction and negates the odds. It further creates interest and the feeling of worthiness.

Knowledge about Human Psychology

As already explained, interrogation involves two sets of individuals with opposite objectives, one wants to save himself while the other determined to implicate. Thus a proxy war prevails, each one tries to outwit the other. The competency is measured by evaluating the performances. It is the mind not the muscle found to be the determining factor. The techniques and pattern of interrogation also depend upon the analysis made of the subject. Human beings are bound by and controlled with divergent compulsions. There are few analogies of which individuals have less or absolute no control. There are lots of stimulations and varied in nature. In interrogation non-verbal communication and body-language also do speak of which we have separately discussed. Whatever might be the mental strength and formation, soon after the apprehension the easiness of the individual evaporates. Bewilderness engrosses him and his state of mind becomes disturbed and perplexed. Tranquility of the subject may or may not surface. It is the tact, talent and experience of the interrogator which could help in rapport building process.

Language Proficiency

A very expected qualification of an interrogator is his proficiency in the language spoken and understanding. Language often becomes a barrier. In these cases, services of interpreter could be utilized. Courts may also be requested in case of any foreign or rarely used languages in our country. Often the Union Home Ministry and Ministry of External Affairs are approached in placing a qualified language expert in that particular case. The problem also arises when the subject remain uneducated and adopted to the local colloquial dialect only. Whatever might be the case, interrogator should interact with the subject in such a fashion which could be understood and the subject should reasonably be able to put his answer. The language should be simple and within the reason evoking sense of the subject. Interrogators having proficiency in the mother tongue of the subject would definitely have edge and command. Knowledge and expertise over the language are, thus, another qualification which an interrogator should possess.

Knowledge about Local Laws

Knowledge about the topography, local customs, conventions, laws and other such prevailing guidelines are also among the required qualifications of an interrogator. India is a country with divergent bickerings and each province dictates their individual terms. Common codes are there but local laws also prevail. While dealing with interrogation, these local laws and practices come in the way. Therefore, the necessity of having specific knowledge on these subjects too.

Patience

Interrogation has got no short cut way, often it prolongs. Therefore the need to have patience. Interrogators with cool and analytical mind and with endurance of having patience are much successful in this process of investigation. One cannot expect that a hardened criminal or anyone knowing fully the punitive aspect of the crime committed by him to come out with the truth easily. Thus the provisions of police remand. Interrogation may go for days and the tussle of patience goes on. The will, determination and the conviction of the interrogators, thus, must not be compounded with any limitations, specially of time. Often a complain is forwarded by the interrogators about the paucity of time. This problem cannot be accepted as interrogation is a team work and a continuous process, till embarkment on a decision. Patience, thus, do play a cognigent role in this process. Power of working hard and withstanding of pressure are other qualities of a good interrogator.

Self Confidence

Confidence is regarded as the mother of any success. Individuals with flickering mind and attitude cannot make a leader. In the context of interrogation, the self confidence of the interrogator is regarded as the corner stone of achieving the success. Confidence is emanated from training, practice and by dint of experience. It is the mental power which creates force and promotes impulses in the minds of the interrogators. Thus potentiality further invokes stamina and strength to overcome all the projected obstacles and counters. It is the mental phenomenon responsible to personify and glorify an individual. Absence of this overture, in interrogation, cows down the subject. Thus the potentiality of this significant power inherited by any interrogator.

Inquisitive Mind

Interrogation is not a stale subject. Each case facilitates new knowledge and skill. Without the driving force like to "earn further", the matter would have, by now, thrown to the dark room. It is the promotion and new adventurism which besieged. Anticipation, imagination, mirror imaging, etc. are also involved in this episode. It is the thrust to learn, the inquisitive mind and the positive endeavour of the interrogator which are of immense importance. Those interrogators having these thinking, anticipating and cultivating tendencies, are recognized as the prudent class in the investigation process. Inquisitiveness may take a case to such unknown and never-predicted areas, which later may be a topic of reference. It not only makes a case livid but also ignites interest in the psyche of the interrogators. Drive and hunch are further matters of interest inherited in it. Inquisitiveness destroys amateurism and casualness too. Keenness, penetration and focusing are emanated from it. The more you are inquisitive, the more you are progressive.

Acting ability/born actor

Interrogators are regarded as born actors. The role played by them, in case to case, transform their abilities and endurance besides skill and perfection. While any police officer is engaged in interrogation, he should be able to act in the role which he is supposed to play in that particular case. Cover means and includes assumed personality. This personality should be such that could convincingly be displayed, without any exposure, and also be quite operational till the culmination of the operation. Interrogation is also considered as an operation, vowed to extract the truth imbibed in the case. Acting is a specialized art. The performance and postures, tackling, flexibilities, concern and handling the situation are matters which require practices. The ability should be such that could charm and crumble the subject.

Patient Listener

Interrogation is a two-way traffic though normally it evolves around question-answer series. One of the most sought after quality of any potential interrogator is his cultivation of listening power calmly and patiently. In interrogation, projection of interrogator's own view has got very limited scope. The demand is oriented around obtaining the correct statement of the subject by this process. His views, comments and descriptions relating to the case under reference are weighing much what the interrogator possesses. It is, more or less, interrogee's version. Thus, he should be allowed to speak freely, elaborately and if possible without any hindrance. The role of the interrogators centre around creating an urge or provoke him to speak on the line. The more he will speak, chances of mistakes, confusions and falsehoods be greater. Interrogator should, being a patient listener, concentrate and attend on the revelations made. He may also take note of the cognitions and mistakes which, later on, be put to dislodge the subject. The subject may be killed by his own bullets. Talkativeness is the human tendency. Therefore, the quality to patiently listen to the revelations made by the subject, is obviously going to pay a good dividend in this criminal investigation process. Another beauty inherited in this is once spoken by the subject, would be difficult to erase. The interrogator by dint of his mastery of the power to quietly listen, would use the "noted avertures" against his enemy. The dictum is speak less and listen more.

Ready Wit

Interrogation is a process with many bindings and permutations. It should never be counted as an unending process though the saying goes, "it has no, end". Therefore while the interrogation process is on, each and every ground should be covered with acute attention so that no vital point is missed. During the courses, many unwanted, irrelevant and even relevant questions may come up from interrogee's side, which require to be answered without involving lengthy thought process. The role of ready wit, thus, is significant in this process. Spontaneisity and the simplicity of the reply forwarded by the interrogator should not evoke any suspicion in the mind of the subject. This tactness sidelined many quarries which the interrogators are not supposed to part with the criminals. In putting vital questions in a very plausible and simple way, ready wit plays significant role. This inherent quality of the interrogator is reckoned to be one of the most essential qualities which every interrogators should display. Opposite to ready wit is flambleness which is likely to go in favour of the subject. Ready wit does not involve falsehood or lying but tactfully sidelining the required answer. If fact, keenness, attention and proper focus on the subject help in ready wit building process besides knowledge on criminology and proper evaluation of the case vis-a-vis the subject. It also helps in quick rapport building as the intelligence of the interrogator bonnets the confidence of the subject.

Alertness

A highly demanded quality. During the process many unforeseen problems and variety of questions may crop up and therefore, the interrogator's alertness, concentration on the total proceedings and each counts are required to be paid attention. Alertness is a must to unearth and further question on each contradictions, wrongs and evasions made. If alertness is not maintained, then there are possibilities of many vital omissions. Alertness also be maintained to count and measure physical condition and verbal and non-verbal communications of the subject.

Courage

Courage is a mental phenomenon which emboldens an interrogation to face and counter forceful challenges posed by dreaded subjects. Diehard criminals, militants, terrorists, persons of high positions, etc. are hard subjects. Therefore, the need of courage component. Courage produces conviction and determination. It further advances the systemic procedures. Interrogator's courage is an essential component. Cowards have got no place in this process. Threats are bound to come and thus one has to overcome these threats and pronouncements.

Unbiased Mind

Interrogators should be free from any kind of biasness. They must study the case in the preparation stage including the observations made in the initial report but when they shall take up interrogation, would be without any pre-conceived idea. They should be void from both internal (official) and external (political/social) influences. Pre-conceived ideas may twist the contour of the case and may lead to wrong direction. Each interrogation is a fresh case. Therefore, earlier experiences may or may not be suitable. Personal grudge, enmity, fellow-feelingness, closeness, religious affinity, social bondage, relationship, comradeship, etc. have no place in this critical and analytical criminal investigation process. Perceptions may differ. It is an impartial game played for national interest and no personal implication is involved. Doing proper justice and garnering of the truth are the basics.

Good Conversationist

Conversation is the base upon which entire standing of interrogation rests. Interrogation is an art of questioning. It is rather founded on questions - answers. It is not a monologue. The urge is for proper and continued dialogue in a systematic and required manner. Conversation is thus the base. Interrogators, therefore, be a good conversationist. His art and tact would evoke interest, urge and provocation in the mind of the subject. His overt silence, if any, may be broken. Thus the requirement of this fundamental component.

Honesty and Integrity

Honesty and integrity are the foundations upon which the moral predicament of any person is gauged. There are many odd forces and influences surrounded around. Each individual has his need and aspiration. Greed and temptations are also there. Uprightness, purity and wholeness are few elements which constitute oneself as professional. These all are components for proper display at the right juncture. Interrogators are also required to harbour all these good qualities in order to prove their worth and create a respectable position. National interest must overcome personal needs, if any.

Team Spirit

Interrogation is a team work and the entire outcome is regarded as the team achievement. Coordinated effort, therefore, is an essential requirement. Better understanding, cohesion and relationship matter much in this serious natured investigation process. Interrogation is void from rank consciousness and other such officialdoms. All are equal players. Know not who would be dear and near of the subject. It's the rapport building quality. Oneness i.e. team work and spirit should be maintained till the culmination. It is not prudent to use terms like "sir", "subordinate", "call by rank" and even by name. Official decorum may be maintained but not at the cost of the spirit of the process. Another cogent point should be kept in mind that in this process there exists no competitive edge. "I am the best" tendency must be buried aside. Gain or loss whatever may be the outcome, shares and bestow upon the team not on the shoulder of any particular interrogator. Rewards and appreciations are also equally shared. Personal envy has to be avoided. The subject may project his interest to anyone of his choice. Team spirit and dignity are, therefore, among the most demanding requirements.

Knowledge about limitation

Interrogators should know where to stop and how far to be stretched which may be termed as limitation of the game. The expectation of the interrogators would not always match with the information revealed by the subject. Moreover stress and other mental factors might stand on blocking the memory as such. The subject may also be privy to certain percentage of the total incident or case. It is otherwise not so easy to remember all the minute details like the dates and times. Therefore, the power or consideration of limitations. Expert interrogators knit the case after ascertaining even sliced facts.

Perfect Memory

Memory plays an essential qualification. Interrogators ability to conduct any interrogation highly depend upon his strong memory and recapitulation power. The sequence of the case and gradual penetration rely on memory. Moreover, anticipation and connecting a case with earlier cases are also product of sharp memory. During the course of interrogation consultation in front of the subject is not desirable and as such one has to depend upon the memory. However, at breaks he can go for consultation and even checking of the records. Sharp memory and timely recapitulation are among the essential qualities of a good interrogator.

Therefore we can conclude that an interrogator must possess all the good qualities an individual of repute should have. He must have intellectual curiosity and must cultivate an interest on the subject and even general aspects. He should be bold and efficient enough to carry out the business smoothly. He should be able to handle any type of subject. He should be a self-controlled, unbiased and a person void of any boosting or bluster. A cool tempered but a tough officer having dominating personality, knowledge, experience and skill. His communication power and convincing ability should be above board. He should also be a law abiding, strict disciplinary and a hard working individual having perseverance.

3 Techniques of Interrogation

Search for a reliable means to identity the untrustworthy is as ancient as man. Human beings are rational animals. The crime components in varying degrees are, thus, inherent in nature and also subjected to modifications. In earlier days some techniques were found in superstition, religious belief, moral chastity, etc. These means were trial by combat. It was then changed to "trial by ordeal" and further to "trial by torture". As already explained, since the evolution of the society and the induction of crime therein, interrogation became a highly used methodology to ascertain the truth and book the real culprits. In ancient China (1000 BC) a particular technique i.e. to allow the suspected individual to eat rice and thereby by measuring the saliva content, the subject's complicity used to be determined. If the rice become wet, the subject used to be truthful. The conception is liar's mouth remains dry. Automatic nervous system inhibits salivation and digestive process when an individual is under serious threat. Interrogation is a battle of wits and a game played by rational animals. In both the sides human factor prevail. The interrogee maybe one, a single individual but his knowledge, skill, training, intelligence may overshadow the faculty of entire interrogation team members positioned against him. The success or failure of the process entirely rely on the technique or methodology adopted by the interrogating team vis-a-vis the tough posture adopted by the interrogee, specially his defensive attire. In interrogation there is no fixed or prescribed technique applicable for all the cases or subjects. But there are few tested techniques, which are detailed below. Another significant point to remember is that in one case one particular technique may yield positive result, while it is not certain that in all the alike cases, this particular technique would produce effective response. It differs from subject to subject, case to case. The prime factor is sizing up and rapport building with the subject. Perfect case study, proper planning and preparation, collection of the background and other antecedents of the subject, unearthing his weakness and strength (strong points), mental conditions of the subject, etc. are few determining factors upon which the adoptability of the technique is bestowed. In other words, the proper study of the subject open up avenues of access. The experience, knowledge, skill, merit and mirror imaging of the interrogators are the major components, which determine the adoptability of the particular technique with the object to break the subject.

The few techniques are detailed below considering their high success rate :

Emotional Appeal

Human beings harbour different behavioural patterns in them. Whatever might be the overt gesture and posture, "emotion" is a component in existence in them. Three main components, as described by the behavioural scientists are ID, ego and emotion. Sudden apprehension produce shock, bewilderment and mental confusion in the mind of the subject. He remains in stress and suffers from emotional discharges, though there may not be much overt manifestations. A tactful interrogator searches for such avenues in quest of his desire to further chanellise the emotional discharges of the subject. In fact the process aims to provide solace to the interrogee. This psychological treatment assuages the inner feelings, the subject finds a friend in distress and finally he develops confidence on the interrogator. While adopting or playing with these techniques, the interrogators should invariably be very calculative, questions should be measured and in every step subject's reaction should be noted and examined.

Keep him waiting

Let the interrogee be seated alone in the interrogation room. There should not be any interrogator within his visual range. This long waiting is likely to produce many bickerings in his mind, which is likely to create mental turbulence and pressure. This state of mind shall further aggravate with the increase of stress and strain. If the subject is a patient of high blood sugar or high/low blood pressure, the pressure ratio is likely to shoot up. The deceptiveness of the subject, if any, is likely to be affected and the defensive mood of the subject may disappear owing to long spell of waiting hours. This technique is nothing but to allow the subject to have soliloquy with himself. The time spell of waiting has to be determined by the interrogators adjusting their requirement. The movements and activities of the interrogee may be quietly monitored through clandestine CCTV coverage.

Rapid Questioning

Rapid, continuous, sharp and unabated showering of questions by the interrogators are bound to create confusion and impact in the mind of the interrogee. The questions of various types are simultaneously put by individual interrogators whereby the subject find no time to prepare answer of his own and is rather forced to cater replies almost spontaneously. He is also denied to build defensive answers. Moreover, he looses consequences and he is often not able to remember what all he answered earlier. He is, thus, trapped. The fallout of this well chalked out technique is vomiting of truth, though inadvertently. Where the entire proceedings are recorded, the relevant portion, if required, may be played before the subject. This technique proves to be very potent where the subject adopt deceptiveness from the very beginning and acute self-defensive in nature.

Human Appeal

As explained earlier, in interrogation game both the interrogee as well as the interrogators are human beings. The former may be an offender while the latter are the custodians of the law and order. Interrogee is obviously in distress, often helpless and lonely. His state of mind may not be stable too and he may suffer from various kinds of mental agonies and pressures. Human touch and inter-personal relationships are desired treatments. It is better not to treat the subject as a convict or prisoner. Hate the sin not the sinner, an ancient saying goes. In fact, according to legal definition, he cannot be treated as a prisoner till he is convicted. Soft handling, making queries about his health condition, family affairs and other such personal matters may help in quick rapport building. Friendly initiatives and creating of a congenial atmosphere are likely to pay rich dividend. It is thus a process where the mind of the subject is minutely read and an attempt is made to distract his mind away from the crime scenario. The entire effort is based on human consideration and building up friendship with the focused opponent. This principle is also known as treating the subject a fellow human being. To obtain greater and quick success, knowledge of human psychology and its proper use are core components.

Dodging and de-dodging technique

Anticipation and finally elimination of few commonly adopted dodging techniques by the interrogee primarily to buy time and secondarily to evade interrogation (they even well calculate the remand period). Projections of unsound health, mental illness, lack of memory, loss of remembrance, denying his knowledge and presence during the crime, etc. are few common attempts tried by the subject to dislodge interrogation for the time being. Often he complains about chest pain and try to get himself admitted in any hospital. He may go on producing series of examples and illustrations, all deceptive in nature, in order to buying sympathy of the interrogators. A tactful interrogator shall listen to him and by way of elimination, he would remove the false alarms raised by the subject. Often subject may pronounce warning citing Human Rights violation. In acute case a fake or tutored doctor be consulted and the subject's dodging attempts be squashed. The convincing and countering abilities of the interrogators are reckoned to be vital in this process.

Persuasive Method

Persuasion technique is generally being adopted to subvert the loyalty of the communists, religious fundamentalists and other such "dogma" based subjects. Continuous hammering on one's ear and prolonged efforts ultimately soften the target and mould his outlook, conviction and belief. This technique is equally productive in interrogation where the continuous and prolonged persuasion of the analytical and school master types of interrogators ultimately toll upon the subject. This effort is nevertheless time consuming, monotonous and worrisome. Tolerance, endurance and sustained capabilities of the interrogators are essential qualities which interrogators engaged in this process should possess.

Brain Washing

As the term denotes, brain is the window of mind. Every individual suffers from ID, ego and superego and few impressions are permanent which are difficult to erase from one's mind. Both physical and mental resistance automatically shoot up and the subject cooks alibis in his defence. Brain plays a significant role. Thus brain needs to be hammered. Interrogation is a psychological warfare in which two opposite minds remain engaged in defeating the other. Continuous and sustained brainwashing of the subject is carried out with the object to bring forth and amend the subject's ideas, actions and conceptions. The negative or restrictive attitude of the subject is reformed with the brainwashing endeavour of the interrogators. Convincing capability and reasoning power are the moving force. Certain categories of subjects suffer from strong convictions and pre-conceived ideas. Once these are sidelined, they become mentally perturbed. Many of the terrorists are initially brainwashed by their leaders. They conceive either a very bleak or absolutely rosy picture. Once the interrogators brainwash these subjects by illuminating the correct posture and position, the sky becomes clear and the interrogee is often repentant. This technique is unique in nature. It not only compels the subject to subjugate and reveal the truth but later on this subject may be utilized in countering the purpose and object of the organization. Brainwashing methodology is not a new phenomenon, it was in vogue in ancient times too.

Focusing light on the Face

Focusing of powerful lights on the face of the interrogee are aimed to irritate the subject as well as to cause physical discomforts. The system remains in-built in the interrogation room. In this method, the interrogators remain in dark, while the strong lights are focused mainly over the face of the subject. This lighting effect causes direct effect and finally the subject do surrender before the interrogators. During this process, the interrogators continuously remain busy in asking significant questions. The subject fails to withstand this physical torture, which affect both the body and the mind. Care and perfection are required so that accurate hit is engrossed. Subject's hands may be tightened to deprive him to cover his face. Precautions should be taken to prevent any burn injury. In spite of the fact that this procedure is covered under torture as prescribed by the Rightists, system has not yet been stopped.

Sympathy by itself

This method is creating of all friends together situation and roping the sympathy of the interrogee. The interrogators advance cordial, soft, polite and touchy attitudes towards the subject may broche official atmosphere too. A friendly and congenial touch demolishes all the mental blocks and deceptive postures. Once the subject is moulded towards the interrogator, the latter then can tactfully and slowly reach in the inner circle of the subject's mind. Subject develops trust and confidence over the interrogator and he does not hesitate to reveal vital inputs to his opponents. This method requires interrogator's prudency and sharpness in analyzing the mental strength and bickering of the subject. However, the command and control shall rest with the interrogators.

Water Torture

A very simple and age-old method used to break the abrupt silence of the subject. In this method the subject is roped to a chair and over his head a water-container is fixed in such a manner that a drop of water falls on the head of the subject at several second's interval. It is a torture method causing lot of irritation, physical discomfort and annoyance. It stimulates him too. Falling of water (water dropping) over the immovable head ignite lot of tension in the mind too. Final outcome of this cruel method is just submission of the subject before the interrogating team. This process is also reckoned to be a torture but void of any physical torture sign or mark.

Feeding lot of Liquids

Allowing the subject to consume liquids like water, tea, coffee, cold drinks, etc. make him uncomfortable. Feeding of watery substance would automatically fill his bladder and pressure would be mounted to urinate. Subject's appeals to allow him to go for urination would be delayed on the ground of forwarding correct answers. The pressure mounted might force him to disclose the "unwilling part".

Mutt and Geff Technique

This technique has been named after the inventors of this methodology. The process is very easy and simple. Advance planning and preparations are required. Acting abilities of the interrogators are core components. In this method one interrogator presents himself as being harsh, tough and unsympathetic and the other a sympathetic and soft. The subject automatically turns towards the second interrogator who, according to him, may be friendly, saviour and develops intimacy with the second one avoiding the first one.

Continuous Focus

Paying of proper and continuous attention towards the subject, develop positive markings in the psyche of the interrogee. Prolonged, protected and uninterrupted focus engineer pressure and finally the subject breaks. This method also helps in controlling, checking and understanding the interrogee who is left with little scope to conceal his verbal, symbolic and non-verbal communications and certain other gestures. This technique puts more psychological pressure than that of physical one. Continuous attention may also create nervousness.

Right Approachability

Determination of innocence or guilt part is the core object of interrogation. One should not loose sight of the negative side of the process. The approach, therefore, should be focused in right direction and the goal of the concerned interrogation should also be kept in view. Mistaken identity or the incorrect reporting is another confusing factor. The interrogee would be allowed to express himself and to spell about his correct position. Any stern or adamant step or attitude of the interrogators may jeopardize the entire case. It may also provide scope to the actual offenders to escape from the dragnet. Thus right approachability is another technique by way of which the subject is cornered and twisted.

Hurt Thyself

Hate the sin not the sinner. Direct attacks on subject's reputation, honour, dignity, social status, political line up, image and self-respect, the most weakest pressure points, are nevertheless irking points too. The interrogee, who is conscious about his own standings, when hammered on these sensitive issues, is likely to temporarily oblivate his own standing and the "hidden inputs" or "guarded information" may likely to surface. This pumping technique confirms the acting ability of the interrogator.

Shifting of the Blame

The subject remains well abreast of his involvement and complicity in the crime. He is also afraid about punitive measures. While initiating interrogation, the reference be preferred towards involuntarily or accidental commissioning of the crime. Circumstances may also be referred to. Blame may also be shifted to the co-accused or abettors. This technique may provide some solace in the mind of the subject and he may also feel comfortable. This technique helps in quick rapport building and finally breaking the subject.

The hypothetical crime Technique

In this method, a similar (simulated) crime scene is prepared and the subject is taken there. His very visit and witnessing of similar event are likely to evoke repulses. He is then questioned on relevant points. At the pretence of writing down details of the simulated or hypothetical scene of crime, he is evaluated. There remain chances to mingle between the actual and hypothetical scene of crime. He is, thus, trapped.

Scene of crime visit

This technique provides retrieval of lost memory and creating impulses in the mind of the subject by witnessing the scene of crime. His strong defence formation gets jerked. He becomes mentally perturbed and suffers from psychological pressure too. The technique is fruitful in the case of first time offenders, white coloured criminal and children.

Undermining confidence level

Undermining the confidence and distancing the subject from firm determination is a technique adopted in extracting truth. Continuous counselling and persuasion create deep impressions in the mind and psyche of the subject. It is the confidence level, which provides scope for building strong resistance power. Once confidence is destroyed, the entire defence line gets swamped. While sizing up the subject, his level of confidence and convictions also need to be gauged.

Putting up assumptive questions

The entire process rests on professional acumanship and farsightedness of the interrogator. The knowledge, experience and intelligence are also recognising factors. Putting up assumptive or anticipating questions are undertaken to test the reaction of the subject. Abrupt and unforeseen assumptive question not only unnerve the interrogee but also put him in a state that his activities have been exposed. He feels that the interrogators have been able to ascertain the truth and he has got no other way but to admit the guilt. This suspicion may produce lot of verbal and non-verbal communications too.The thinking process of the interrogators thus help in extracting the guilt.

Mirroring

Copying of other's behaviour pattern is known as mirroring. It is used in rapport building process. Neurolinguistics, which is essentially language of the mind is the core component of this method which was first invented by John Grinder, a linguist and Richard Brandler.

Wounded bird play

A diversionary tactic used by an interrogee to lead the interrogator away from the topic that the subject does not want to discuss. Thus when this technique is adopted by the interrogee, effort may be made to countermin it and bring the subject on line. Subject should not be allowed to dictate and take control of the process.

Good guy/bad guy approach

In this type of confrontation with the subject, one interrogator plays a heartless, tough and ruthless role by projecting his physical postures, uttering filthy and abusive language at the highest peak of his voice, on the contrary another interrogator play soft, sobre, sympathetic and compromising role. The former is known as "bad guy" while the latter is termed as a "good guy" owing to their mannerism and attitude towards the subject. Obviously, the subject would try to be close to the good guy and the rapport building endeavour may be faster. The reaction of the subject and the tactfulness of the good guy type interrogator are key points of success. Acting ability of both the interrogators is much accountable in this process.

Veteran Offenders

Dealing with non-emotional offenders who are mostly seasoned, veterans, repeaters, and not emotionally surcharged are really difficult. They are normally not guilty- conscious, but they are usually afraid of being punished. The crime possessiveness of these subjects require acute and factual study by the interrogators to corner them not by reasoning but with the circumstantial evidences and other related facts. Once they are sized up, the dealing bocomes smoother. The toughness and cover story projected by them at the initial stage have to be sidelined by adopting tactical move by the interrogators.

Confusing interpretation of body language

Confusing the subject by pointing his physiological effects, of which he has no control, is another technique. Majority of the subjects accelerate pulsation in the neck. An intelligent interrogator may embark on the psyche of the subject by opining that the prolonged suppression of the truth is the route of putting pressure on carotid artery in the neck causing the continuous perspiration. This indication and the result are medically tested and acknowledged, be stated in clear terms convincing the subject to release his tension for his own betterment. This technique may act on the subject and he may, by telling the truth, release his tension and save himself from further physical complications.

Friend and enemy approach

The friendly role and the unfriendly attitude of two individual interrogators run side by side in order to create an impact in the mind of the interrogee. The "friend" would try to bestow his sympathy, apathy and touch while the "enemy" would continuously blister warning, threats, harshness, condemnation, etc. This equal and opposite balance technique is bound to create an impulse in the mind and thinking process of the subject, who is likely to avoid the "enemy" and be closer to the "friend".

General to specific

Another common process is to start discussing about the general crime scenario of the area without initially touching the specific crime i.e. the topic of the case. Gradually, the subject may be drawn towards the specific crime sequence. In this case also general and non-accusatory matters need to be discussed to provide a feeling in subject's mind that he is not being touched. This process consumes time but ultimately the subject is concerned.

Alibi breaking

Needless to point out that the subject built his defence by consolidating alibi. Plausible alibis are difficult to break. But sustained effort concentrating on a particular point makes the subject weak and reduces his resistance power. This technique is a battle between resistance and hammerings. The prudent, controlled and prolonged approach might break even the well chalked alibi.

Spotting the weak

In case of group arrests or more than one arrest, picking up the weakest is the technique. Screening may be conducted and the weakest one may be interrogated first. Once he reveals the truth, it would be easier to grill others. In order to evaluate any case, the interrogation of the weakest is proposed. Once the real fact is made known, others would find difficulties to disown it. Taped conversations may, if necessary, be played to unnerve others. Last resort is face to face confrontation.

Misquote answers

Proper attention to be paid on any misquote answers. The interrogators should not swallow such answers. Sustained questioning be done, till proper reply is ascertained. Questioning should be rapid, repeated and pointed. Pressure be mounted to fill in the blank.

Talk less, Listen more

The subject may be allowed to speak more and a patient hearing is required. The more he will talk, the more mistakes he is likely to commit. An intelligent interrogator collects cues from the deliberations made by the subject. He is systematically and effectively be grilled on each such utterings of his own. It becomes difficult on his part to contradict his own utterings and he has to submit.

Cornering by evidence

At planning and preparation stage it is compulsory to examine each and every recoveries made. These are invariably examined further with the subject during the course of interrogation. He is liable to answer all the queries made by the interrogator. In this method he is bound to reveal the truth. Other evidences, if any, may also be projected and vetted. Since these have been recovered from his possession, he is liable to provide correct and convincing replies. He may be warned that non-cooperation would further bind him in the case.

Playing one against the other

Where there are more than one subject, this technique is useful. In this technique one subject is apprised that the other has exposed him. Let's examine his reaction. He is likely to comment adversely against the other subject. Similar way, the other subject may be engaged. The interrogators finally would be able to collect the correct picture.

Give a long rope

Interrogation is a lengthy and sustained effort. Allow the subject to narrate what all he desires to reveal. Just give him a patient hearing. Time shall come when he may be tired and then put questions taking cue from his own revelations. He is likely to be tired. Long time spell has got its own effect.

Confrontations

A very well practised method. In this process subjects are confronted with each others. Both sides would try to shift the burden on the other. The cat, thus, is likely to come out of the bag.

Promoting cooperation through a story

This technique could be adopted when the subject is intelligent and capable of generating good understanding. A story akin to the case under investigation should be narrated and at points comment, opinion and suggestion of the subject be requisitioned in order to gauge his mind, knowledge and complicity. The sequential development and enlarging of the story shall gradually drag the subject's unconscious approach towards the incident. The centrifugal purpose being unconsciously throw the subject in the required dragnet.

Countering interruptions

Deceptive subjects are prone to divert the attention of the interrogators by frequently causing interruptions. Twisting the mood, temper and even fasterness of the process are hindered in a calculated manner. These practices reflect the mindset of the subject too. Interrogators should tactfully avert and sideline these adaptations. These actions are aimed to kill the time, distract attention and focus. Command and control should be with the interrogators.

Behavioural changes

How much resistive the subject may be, in course of forwarding replies, specially denial answers, certain behavioural changes, in his eyes, face, forehead, body language, breathing style, time space, using of words, speech, cohesion, sentence strength, etc. are few abnormal but spontaneous uncontrolled pronouncements of which the subject may even not be aware of. These overtures are keenly be observed and the interrogator should put forward with reasoning before the subject in order to unnerve him. Continuous pressure shall prevail upon and subject would be subjugated to admission stage.

Bluff in a split pair

Where the accomplices are more than one, two of them may be separated. One may be told that the other has spoken implicating about you. You have been framed by him. Purpose is to ignite anger over the other and in this process both are likely to expose and implicate others. In adopting this technique, the interrogator would be able to extract the reality of the case and the actual involvement of each of the accused.

Change of team

Interrogation is a team work and the main object is to break the subject in order to dig out the truth. In the event of one team's inability to gain success in their endeavour, it is suggestive to change the team . The approach and techniques may act upon the subject and the subject is likely to react. New faces, attitude changes, freshness and the approachability may help in nexus and rapport building process. Many times, the subject in spite of his desire to reveal the truth, refrained from opening up owing to tough posture projected by the interrogators. The fear psychosis may likely be changed with the introduction of new faces.

Examination away from the subject's place

Interviewing a subject away from his home or in the area of his domination is a method to deprive the subject to consolidate his mental strength. A man's home is his own castle. He is the boss in his area of operation or pocket of influence. Often criminals are engaged in social works with the ostensible object to garner sympathy and support of the local people. Presence of relatives, friends and associates are encouraging factors and advantageous points to the subject. All these factors embolden his mental strength and are encouraging grids of registering defences. Therefore, the technique to dislodge the interviewee from his own location.

Exposure of the acts displayed during the performance of the crime

Intelligent interrogators inculcate the ability to draw the case and during interrogation, they display to role played by the interrogee. The interrogators should have the competency to prevail upon and convince the subject his ability to "walk a mile" in other's shoes, to feel the stress and the fear involved in the episode. He continues to expose the conditions, behavioural changes, guilt reflection in his face and many such signs. This process, however, may consume time to develop guilt sense in him.

Thematic Appearception Technique

Thematic Appearception Test (TAT) is a psychological test introduced by Raymond Morgan. It is a projective examination where an individual is shown vague sketches and asked to built a story out of them. The very construction of the purported sketch is made in such a fashion that the entire backdrop, involvements, actions and the ending of the crime under investigation are relayed. The subject while building or narrating the story expectedly mingled up his own imagination with the actual happenings inadvertently. Morgan, however, divided the sketch in four parts, namely relevant, guilt, remorse and apprehension cards. These cards are made gender-specific and are developed step by step in a systematic way to corner the subject in outwitting his deceptive tendencies. The entire procedure may take about five minutes and this time restriction would not allow the subject to incubate dodging tendencies.

CONCLUSION

Few accepted techniques, discussed above, are not enough to cover the entire gamut of interrogations. The varieties, diversities and characteristics of the subjects and the wide-angled crime perpetrations might not allow to involve a particular technique or method. The manner, mode and modality should suit the case and the subject. Innovative mind, search for new ideas, inhibition, conceptuality and power of improvisions might oblivate ganglion attitude fostered by the interrogee. Demands for new methods and techniques are there to cope with the developing crime contours and crime horizons. Kaleidoscoping change is inevitable and welcome. The research and studies are on. The inquisitiveness and professional zeal of the interrogators would crush this threat (i.e. breaking the subject) and would solve this puzzling problem. With the advancement of science and technology and with the growth of human faculties, there are likelihood to emancipate from the hindrances projected by the interrogee with the birth of new techniques.

FEW SPECIAL TIPS FOR THE INTERROGATORS

1. One should be mentally prepared and he should be free from any kind of interferences. Clear mind is an essential element. The clearness of one's mind shall generate eventful and cogent thinking. It would also help in obstructing stress formation. Any preoccupation should not stand in the way.
2. Please check whether all members of your team are trained in interrogation tradecraft. If you intend to include any trainee interrogator in your team, he should be adequately briefed, specially about the role played by him during the process.
3. Prior to taking part in any interrogation, one should check his dress, materials carried by him and should have a pen and a pocket book. If he is carrying MCR, its functioning should be checked. He must carry additional batteries. Medicines or other items of daily habits, should invariably be carried. There must be provision for drinking water and tea at breaks. None should carry open weapon. However, the security guards should carry arms and ammunition.

4. Interrogation should be taken as early as possible. The more the delay, shall allow the subject to chalk out strategies for deception. Delay shall also provide opportunities to the co-accused to go underground and to shift arms, ammunition, explosives and also to destroy clues or evidences. Delay may also cause decay in memory too. The interrogee may also send messages to others about the expected fallouts. Delay shall allow time to consult lawyers.

5. It is suggested to choose night specially after 10 p.m. while you are going to interrogate in the Police Station or alike places. After 10 p.m. as normal official interferences subside there exists calmness in the atmosphere. You will feel comfortable in conducting the operation in a congenial manner. Only you have to be more cautious about security placements. If you can discreetly pour more sugar in the tea cup of the subject, that may produce some effect on the subject. In the night it has been observed that more concentration could be reflected.

6. When you are unable to elicit correct reply by posing a single question, put two or three questions simultaneously and break his nerve. The idea behind is to confuse him and bring out desired reply. The nature of the questions and the art of putting up of these questions require pre-thinking.

7. Never project casualness or slip shod manner. From the very beginning the subject should understand that he won't be allowed to let off unless he speaks the truth. This mannerism is always projected by gesture and posture and not by oral depiction.

8. Always remember that time scheduling shall be at your hand. Consume time but economically. Be logical and systematic. Never project hastiness. Even if you are in a hurry, the subject should not be privy to it. Prolonged interrogations have been adversely viewed by the judiciary. They even went on recording it as a torture. However, you are the best judge of the case and the situation.

9. Always try to confuse the subject. The more creation of confusion and bickering, the more the flow of expected revelations.

10. In case of any interview of a witness be conducted, try to isolate him from his home and associates. Witnesses tend to be deceptive when he is in his own area and with his own people. Isolation and privacy shall act upon him. He is likely to reveal the truth. Secrecy part and confidentiality would encourage the witness to speak out the factual details. Fear of exposure and retaliatory action besieged the subject most. Any individual's home is viewed as his castle.
11. Using of any technical devices, specially for monitoring the non-verbal communications and recording of the entire proceedings, would never be within the knowledge preview of the subject. If he remains aware of these monitoring, he is likely to be cautious in utterings.
12. It is advantageous to allow minimum comfort to the subject with the object to keep him normal. Let him feel that he is being treated well. Always project that any non-cooperation shall liable him sufferings. It is nothing but a stress projected on him.
13. At the initial stage never hammer the subject, allow him to free forward lies as much as he can. You can corner him by his own utterings and confront and expose his lies. Once he is proved as a liar, his morality is shaken.
14. It is a fact that the arrested subjects remain under stress. You have to find out the causes. Give him mental solace. Shocking aspect may be removed. Try to be closer to his mind and try to ascertain from him difficulties and problems faced. In case you are in a position to help or assist, may do it. This action of yours would help in rapport building. You are likely to be friendly. In doing all these, your senior officials should invariably be apprised of.
15. One of the object of interrogation is contact raising. By way of your dealing, treatment, behaviour and concern you may develop dependency and trust. The objective of source raising, thus, be kept in view where feasible. Be refrained from creating an enemy.

16. Physical searches of the interrogees, prior to taking up of the process, are precautionary measure. Similarly fresh medical examination of the interrogee is another safeguard to avert any future complication.

17. Operational inputs, ascertained from the subject, need to be shared with the concerned authority without consuming much time. The subject, however, should not be aware of the action taken.

18. Maintaining secrecy is of pivotal need. Restrictive security obligations must also be followed. Refrain from careless and casual conversation or discussions in the presence of any undesirable elements. Press and media people be totally avoided.

19. Interrogators should pay proper heed to writing of the IR It is the report which reflects the potency of the case. One should not make haste or to write the report at random or in improper way. Report writing has been discussed separately and the required procedure should, therefore, be followed. It should not be left to one interrogator. The team, prior to writing final report should discuss pros and cons and the threadbear analysis should also be done. If possible the salient points, in logical and chronological way, may be jotted down.

QUESTIONING

It is suggested that during the preparation stage probable questions may be well thought of and a comprehensive list be prepared. Preparation of this list containing questionnaires may help in two ways, firstly in the preparation stage a comprehensive study would be required on the subject and the case and secondly blocking of chance of missing any interesting question during the course of action. At the end or just prior to the closer of interrogation, if a check is undertaken of the list, the mistaken part can be easily detected. Interrogation is an art of questioning putting up and the veracity of questions matter much. The modalities and techniques of embracing any subject with sharp and well thought pragmatic questionnaires are most meaningful in this operation. Dialogues matter and derive immense significance. The ways and weighing of coining the questionnaires shall depend upon the importance of the case, position of the subject and the relativity and ramification of the offence committed. It remained a fact that majority subjects suffer from mental dis-equilibrium and also remain in a perplexed state of mind. Both their retention and retrieval power may be in a jeopardy. Thus the coinage and framing of the questions should be in such a way which could easily generate reply of the desired kind. Clarity and simpleness are the most demanding components beside the language. The language must be well understood by the subject, preferably using of local dialect. It is prudent not to use any hard or technical word but while replying if the subject offers any "code" or local word, that must be subscribed along with the meaning elaborated in the bracket in English. Questioning requires proper evaluation of the interrogee. His educational, social and cultural standard should be gauged. Age too is a factor such as juveniles require separate elaboration. Different professionals are apt to use special natured words too. Some dialects are likely to pose difficulties in understanding. The tuning and tone may create confusion. Rural area people are used to speak in a different tone than those of the civilized areas. Therefore, much thinking and planning are to be done in preparing questionnaires and also the manner, mode and intensity fixing. The entire pressure and thrust are mounted on the interrogator not upon the interrogee. If the interrogee is unable to understand the meaning of a question put to him, how he would be able to answer it? Framing and delivery are also of equal importance. Putting part by part, logically and systematically might be grasped better purposeful and motivated questions may be avoided at the initial juncture. Beginning may be with common and open natured questions not touching crime part. It is also prudent to avoid "charged words" like murder, rape etc. and also legal words. Punishment and section framed must not be part of questioning. Short, focused questions and elaboration of hypothetical ideas should be forwarded for creating urge to reply.

The purpose of putting questions to a subject is to extract the truth and simply enlightening the inner urge in the mind of the subject so as to reveal what all significant knowledge he is having and part played by him. The focus may also be oriented to expose deceptiveness if adhered to by the subject. Questions and cross question may corner him and thus continuity and prolonging are required in this process. Conversation should continue. Blind question are to be avoided. Inaccuracies, discrepancies, falsehoods, mistakes and dodging should be noted minutely from the free revelations made by the subject. Therefore, the interrogee may be given a long rope i.e. he may be allowed to put forward what all he is interested to share. The more he will talk, the more faultlines are likely to emerge. Problem arises with the reserved type subject who are calculative and cautious in opening up their mouth. Few interrogees prefer to keep mum, silent in their behaviour and forward only very criptive and well thought of answer. They found to be much careful in choosing the word. Putting up of direct question is not permitted. Direct question creates alertness and sensitizes the subject. He, thus, tries to avoid answering of such question. The objective of interrogation is also exposed. Round about questions are safer. Closed end questions are also not prudent. Questions may be short in nature but answer may be elaborated.

Questions should be effective in nature which are likely to focus on the gravity of the offence, elicit the truth and also ascertaining interpretable behaviour of the subject. Each question should refer to a specific issue and required to be repeated till the desired reply is ascertained. Changing of the coinage of the words, i.e. the variation of words are essential component to break the silence of the subject. Monitoring the verbal and non-verbal communications and exposing the "guilt part" may yield positive result. The nervousness of the subject and unnecessary consuming time to reply a question are negative factors of which proper focus of the interrogators should be laid to expose deceptiveness of the subject. The teams should continuously shower questions to unnerve and break the silence of the subject. Appropriate questioning is likely to evoke repulses in the mind and psyche of the subject. Same type of questions, using alternative words may be put by several interrogators and the volley of questions should be continuous to deprive the subject to concentrate much. This process would finally force the subject to utter the truth spontaneously. He may, however, at later stage feel guilty but be roped by the mistakes. Do not forward a too elaborative question. The said question may be processed into small parts. The mental phenomenon and stability of the subject may not be able to part with these lengthy type questions. Moreover, he may get reprieve and choose the suitable part of these questions and dwelt upon the same. The complicated and implicated parts would be avoided.

Controlled questions are those which are akin or close to the direct questions but not directly related to the issues under investigation. Subject may have some behavioural change and he might be attempting to control his deceptive behaviour. He may also be cautious about his body language than that of answering the question. Using of "entice" question is a behaviour provoking one. The normalcy and perceived posture of the subject are required to be over-shadowed and urge to answer the question be provoked. Enticement is nothing but to engineer anger, fury and irritation in the mind of the interrogee. Owing to fit of temper, he is likely to let loose the deceptive pressure so long reserved by him. Non-accusatory questions would entice the subject to change or twist the fact involved in the case. He is most likely to change his earlier revelations and thereby would create trap for himself. Intelligent interrogators put onus upon the subject to select the correct one. An enticement question can also be used to overcome weak denials or to enhance the interrogator's ability to develop the admission of the subject. These types of questions are cooked by the experienced interrogators to emit pressure.

It is unwise to put blunt, curt or complexed questions when the subject found cooperative. These natured questions may irate him and may also provoke him to be hostile. Similarly, at the very outset abusive languages be avoided. Soft questioning and slow but steady mannering do help in rapport building. Never put careless questions which might belittle the interrogator's image. The purpose of questioning to a subject is to amplify certain points and to further the process of investigation. The elements of the offence and other guiding point may form part of questioning. Questions are the basis of prolonging and guiding the conversation. Therefore, the prime focus should be on accurate and positiveness. Odd questions are made with the objective to break the silence only. Once the conversation is in progress, then economy of the timing should be priotarized. Questions should also be in the nature of corroboration and to fill the inaccuracies. These are also part of collection of intelligence, data and future course of actions or targets. Few reports are also evaluated through questionings. Discrepancies, moles, falsehood, mistakes, lacunas, gaps and organizational weaknesses are other most serious topics of questioning. The output of the questioning i.e. the verbal revelations made are always subject to corroboration or vetting and thus several measures are undertaken including hammering the interrogee on the point from all probable angels. Often hypothetical ideas are built and questions are generated in order to reach to the focused area.

Types

Questions may be of various types and shall depend upon the gravity of the case and personal profile of the interviewee or interrogee. Few of them are briefly detailed below:

Relevant : Relevant questions are those which have direct bearing in the case concerned. Selection of these questions require good home working, intelligence and experience. These questions are put only after proper rapport building and in a very cautious way.

Irrelevant : Irrelevant questions are necessarily put to initiate a dialogue, to break the composure of the subject and to create an urge to speak. These questions too require apt selection.

Opened end : Questions replies of which are elaborative and the interrogees would be forced to dwelt at length. Reasoning and forwarding of arguments do form part of the replies. Subject just cannot close his mouth.

Closed end : Closed end question warrant criptive reply. Assertions are positive or negative in nature. The answer centres around either accepting or negativating the guilt part. Close end questions are normally not used while the process is hot.

Direct bearings : Questions which form part of the evidence. The answers have got evidential connotation. Forms part of admission too.

Leading questions : Interrogation tradecraft prohibits an interrogator to put any leading question to the interrogee. Overtly this precautionary or preemptive measure deprives a subject to gauge the interest of the interrogator. "A question is a leading one, when it indicates to the witness the real or supposed fact which the examiner expects and desires to have confirmed by the answer" [Rational of Judicial Evidence — by Betham]. In majority cases question is asked only to receive positive or negative answer i.e. "yes" or "no" forms. Sometimes the limitation is orbited to receive only affirmative reply. But any question asked to a witness to ascertain whether or not, is not covered under the meaning of the leading question. The desired answer is the main focus together with the reference and gravity of the answer. Broad and flexible character of the answer are other points of determination.

DECEPTION

Deception is an inherent tendency of human being and it is embodied in the very nature of any human being, whatever may be his or her status. It is the education, environment and the society which create influence and mould a subject. By deception we mean concealing the truth, a dodging tendency, hiding or disguising the truth. Problem arises when we fail to distinguish or separate "harmless lie" from the "harmful ones". Lies do not necessarily represent complete distortion of realities. Truth is defined as the deliberate, complete and objective communication, may be verbal, written or by gesture, of the recollection of a person, place, thing and/or event, which the communicator believes to exist, have existed or occurred. The definition of a lie is just opposite. As we grow, we learn from the school, family and the society the moral and ethical contour of telling a lie. Lying may be by omission and commission. Fabrication and pouring colour over any incident run from man to man. People engaged in these processes, obviously suffer from psychological heightening.

Here we are concerned about the behaviour of the criminals so as to their association or connection in a particular crime is concerned. A good interviewer or interrogator is destined to dig out the truth. The subject too would try to outwit the interrogator with their deceptive endeavours till they can persist. They mainly suffer from fear and are also apprehensive of stringent punishment. Deceptive people always estimate an interrogator a superior one who would, by adopting techniques, overpower them and thus from the very beginning a tough posture of deception is adopted by them. Anxiety, future prognosis and the "dark past" are other factors. Past experience of the veteran criminals, high degree of motivation, religion's oath and fear of retaliatory actions even to the family members too are other factors promoting deceptiveness.

Physiological and psychological processes of a deceptive subject, if minutely observed and examined, the truth could be substracted. The central nervous system creates a mechanism, which may be termed as "fight or flight". In this mechanism, the body involves in a perceived threat attacking and affecting him and his future, and thereby relates to either stand and fight or flee the threat. The inner conflicts produce nonverbal and psychological order which an experienced interrogator explores in his favour. Deceptive subject's breathing, heart rate, cardiac output, looks and body language produced "exited metabolism". Mind and memory functions to harbour incoherence owing to persistent threat prevailing in the psyche of the subject. Truth is the deliberate, complete and objective communication, whether verbal, written or by gesture, of the recollection of a person, place, thing or event which the communicator believes to exist, have existed or occurred. Deception or lie is just the opposite. Deception is to hide the truth or disguise the truth. In other societies these persons are untrustworthy. Deceptive suspects are also called as "rustle" and they lost their credibility too.

Deception is, a major threat in interrogation process. Thus, the tough posture, understanding of all the relevant facts and fictions, sizing up of the interrogee and strong professional competency of the interrogator are essential elements in thwarting this tendency. Once deceptiveness is removed, the actual process of generation of information shall start. Exhortations to tell the truth for the sake of truth, moral well being and religion may often yield positive results with the first offenders or subjects with a feeling of remorse. But equally a seasoned or veteran criminal or the highly indoctrinated terrorists or militants shall not be easy to be subjugated. Their deception capabilities, building and sustaining of the covers and alibis are tough to be broken. Nervous subjects need soft, systematic, slow and steady tacklings.

Another important point involved may be, deception not done with a motive but lack of observation, incorrect knowledge or partial knowledge, low intelligence and lack of education may also force a subject to be deceptive.

Reasons

There are several reasons why a subject adopt deceptibility and try to resist confession? Few of them are discussed below :

1) *Fear of arrest:* The subjects who have not yet been shown formal arrest and are called on suspicion for interrogation/ interview, try initially to hoodwink the interrogators claiming themselves as innocents. Their object remains to dodge the interrogators by cautiously replying each question and buying time. Fear of arrest make them panicky.
2) *Fear of prosecution:* Once the crime is made open, and the quantum of punishment became known, subject's tendency remain to dodge implication and thereby avert punishment.
3) *Fear of embarrassment:* is the other factor. Specially socially acknowledged persons, persons having self-image and men of high positions do respect their positional image. They tend to keep these and thereby prepare a solid mental preparation. Often they adopt counter-questioning techniques to impress and control the interrogators.
4) *Fear of termination:* Subjects may be reluctant to make an admission because it may affect his job or employment. As a matter of rule if any government employee remains under police custody for more than 24 hours he is liable for suspension till the disposal of the case.

5) *Fear of retaliation:* by his partymen, gang people not only to the subject but also to his family members is another factor. Fear of elimination is also counted as another pressure mounted on the subject.

6) *Financial implication:* is another component for which the subject becomes reluctant to admit his guilt.

7) *Position lost:* Once arrested and if his identity is exposed, his party or organization is likely to distrust him and even expell him from the organization. This fear provokes him and inspires him too, to conceal his real identity.

8) Projection as a role model. Subject by not confessing or even decepting the interrogators, proved his loyalty and ideological indoctrination. After his release he became a hero and a role model to others. Family pressure and threat pronounced by subject's companions, leaders and group members are other significant points in this regard.

9) Education, knowledge and experience of the subject vis-à-vis with the interrogators are also determining factors. Veteran criminals are experienced enough and they are even able to size up the interrogators.

10) Non-supporting environment and paucity of time (of the interrogators) may encourage resistance approach too.

CROSS EXAMINATION

The art of cross examination has ever been considered and emphasized as one of the essential and valuable element and much potent in criminal investigation process. The prime object of cross examination is ascertaining the truth, if not fully, to the extent as could be. There are few procedural technicalities and techniques in the developing of cross examination. This intelligent and imperative art involve lot of studies and experience in order to understand, evaluate the individual concern and the total bearings of the case. The belief that no safeguard for testing the value of human statements is comparable with facts furnished by cross examination, and the conviction that no statement, unless by special exception, should be used as testimony unless it has been proved and sublimated by that test. These have been legally acknowledged as a powerful and valuable weapon to vet and test the veracity, accuracy, motive, tendency and the overall utterings of the witness. A complex and comprehensive picture may arise. It is a common tendency of the human beings to start with falsehood and fabrication and gradually toed towards the real or truth. There may be rare cases where witness may be akin to the truth from the very beginning and he or she may remain strict to their point throughout. Professional liars are also not rare. The method by which the required information and the crime contours are collected is known as cross-examination.

Sec. 137 of the Indian Evidence Act has defined "cross-examination" as the examination of a witness by the adverse party. The examination of a witness by the party who calls him shall be called his examination-in-chief. Sec 138 of the Indian Evidence Act further explains that witness shall be first examined-in-chief, then (if the adverse party so desires) cross-examined, then (if the party calling him so desires) re-examined. By re-examination we mean the examination by the party. The examination and cross-examination must relate to relevant facts, but the cross-examination needs not be confined to the facts to which the witness testified on his examination-in-chief.

Sec 145 of the Indian Evidence Act empowers to call a person for cross-examination who has earlier given a written statement. The purpose of calling this individual is bestowed on the logic that the intention and authenticity should be established. The Indian Evidence Act vide Sections 146 to 154 dealt with the modalities of the questionings and the witnesses responsibilities thereon. Indian Evidence Act has provided enough scope both to the defender as well as the "adverse party" to use this method towards their ends.

Scope

It may be said that the very scope of cross-examination is wide enough to :

i) provide sufficient opportunities to both the parties to confirm their testimonies,

ii) plug any scope of falsehood or deceptiveness,

iii) obtain the full details and truth inherited in it, and

iv) in case of any falsehood or fabrication to expose the same.

It may also be kept in mind that cross-examination is not only aimed to discredit or get rid of the said witness. The basic credit or discredit would be finally evaluated by the court and none else.

Process

The process of cross-examination includes the following angles:

a) Knowledge about criminology and crime investigation procedures.

b) Adequate knowledge about the existing laws, procedures and embargoes (by the judicial pronouncements).

c) Human psychology. Behaviour pattern.

d) Art of winning people. Rapport building.

e) Sizing up and assessment of the individual.

f) Experience and training.

g) Tact, talent and experience of the person/persons involved in this process.

Often it may be a lengthy procedure. Endurance, thus, is a must. One has to create interest and urge so that the necessary replies are emanated. The witty, intelligent and resourceful persons are much successful in this episode.

There are certain norms or indications to ascertain aspiration or doubt upon the witness. These are:

a) When the revelation is beyond the course of nature.

b) When it or these are improbable.

c) Self contradictory.

d) There are inconsistencies.

e) Enmity to the opposite party is proved.

f) Person under cross-examination is found under any threat, intimidation or temptation.

Cross-examination, thus, may yield to :

1) Fully reliable inputs.
2) Partly reliable and
3) Totally false, untrue or fabricated inputs.

Every criminal charge has got two compartments, namely (i) the crime has been committed and (ii) the accused is the author of it. The rule is that no person shall be required to answer or be involved in the consequences of guilt without satisfactory proof of the *corpus delicti* either by direct evidence or by cogent and irresistible grounds of presumption. Criminality, however, never to be presumed. There must be clear and unequivocal proof of the *corpus delicti.*

Cross-examination is carried with an object. Every witness is required to be examined at the earliest possible time so that the memory remains afresh. Recollections of every minute details are much significant. The practice, in vogue, is interviewing a witness by question and answer and then reduce the same in writing. Both the parties and also the trial judge have got statutory opportunities to examine and verify the statements made. The witness should put his signature in the written statement. However, he may later repudiate the statement. An adverse witness hesitates to sign.

While proceeding for any cross-examination the following preparations and studies are mandatory.

i) Assemblage, investigation and analysis of the factual dates.
ii) Detailed note about involvement and role of each individuals.
iii) Known probabilities, affirmative points and other connected positive and negative factors.
iv) Defence likely to be adopted
v) Contradictions, discrepancies, missing links.
vi) Area or points which are requiring elaboration

vii) The nature, relationship and background of the witness.

viii) Charting of obscure and technical points.

ix) Testification of the physical evidence by the witness.

One should stress on methodical preparation of cases and mastery of facts.

Do's and Don'ts in Cross-examination

1) Do not cross-examine without any purpose. There should be an object behind this exercise. Aimless interrogation should be avoided. There ought to be no cross-examination for the sake of examination.

2) Never ask any destructive or reckless question. It may generate adverse effect. It is wiser not to risk by putting a dangerous question.

3) Presumptive questions may be put and the witness should be given a long rope.

4) It is not safer to cross-examine your own witness. Unjustly it may create confusion and may yield disastrous result.

5) Do not insult the witness. However, you may psychologically treat his/her impulses.

6) Divert witness from your gains.

7) It should be done intelligently, logically and systematically.

8) Unwilling and evasive witness should be examined tactfully.

9) Whims better be pushed away.

10) Do not pronounce any threat or warning.

11) Stretch the examination to the level desired. "So far and no further" policy should be adopted.

12) One pertinent question may be put in order to elicit correct reply, on various angles. But once the desired result is gained, it is safer not to repeat it.

13) Do not keep any room for effective and damaging re-examination.

14) Material evidences and other connective statements should be used effectively.

15) Tactical restraint adopted should be thrust out.

16) Language should be used of the level of understanding of the witness.

17) Do not allow the witness to feel that he is being suspected. It is better to leave his inconsistencies or contradictions for argument rather than providing opportunity to explain, wherein he may be able to provide plausible explanation.

18) Strip off the motive. Feeling will impel the liar to deviate from the reality.

19) Diamond cuts diamond, certain lies may be countered by counter lies, and

20) Excitement at the time of observation may be avoided.

COMMUNICATION

Communication is one of the cornerstones of interrogation. Communication, in this intelligence tradecraft, means and includes a bridge of proper understanding and adequate translation of ideas, views and information cue. In this most sordid game both the concerned parties i.e. the interrogee and the interrogators must express and expose their words in such terms, bearings and clarity so that no ambiguousness exits. The contents need to be well understood and free from complications. It may be a two-way traffic. Simplicity, clarity and understandability must be there. That's why in this process using of "hard", "not understood words" are to be avoided. Education level of the subject and his social bearing are also reckoning grids. Communication process should be such that the subject becomes aware of the meaning of the question and the desired information. Communication may, thus, be void from knowledge testing

Interrogation is mostly question-answer series. Therefore, both the concerned parties, from the beginning, play a cautious game. The beauty and brevity are gauged by evaluating communication modes and command and control. In this process the role of the interrogators is much significant. Subjects tend to be deceptive and shall try to evade punishment. They are, in most cases, aware of the consequences of the revelations made. Few may be veteran in crime line and may also be experienced. Threats, circumstantial pressures and inapt handling by the interrogators are few negative aspects to act on the interrogee.

Interrogation is a systematic and well organized process. Therefore, the need of an Interrogation Room which may provide proper communication facilities. There may not be any distraction. The attitude and interest of the interrogators are key factors. The object remains to dig out the truth and in this game they highly depend upon the effective communication. Personality, experience, projections, gestures and postures, question putting abilities, processing of the questions, monitoring and observing the verbal and non-verbal communications of the subject, creating an urge by the interrogators are much needed. It is really a psywar and a battle of outwitting each other. Training and experience do play pivotal role. Looks i.e. the very attitude of the interrogator is vital in this game. Killing looks shall have solid effect. Through the eyes introspection, the interrogator should burn the subject.

Perfect actions and body language of the interrogator are reckoned together with the use of selected, solid, effective and provocative words. One should invariably be polite and polished, specially at the initial stage in order to bridge rapport. Humorous approach may distance away the gravity of the offence. The approach may be audience friendly. In each step and stage, the behaviour of the subject need to be mapped and accordingly questionings be carried out. Performance evaluation should also be simultaneously done. The pressure and interpersonal behaviour pattern would be adjusted accordingly. Smiling face wins friends while tough gesture, since the initiation, may jeopardize the homely atmosphere and provoke the subject to be on guards. Understanding each others is utmostly needed. Both the interrogee and interrogators' communication abilities will generate truth inherent in the concerned case.

4 Third Degree

Torture or violence was widely prevalent in various forms since the Vedic Ages in India. Kautilya's *Arthasastra* described various methods of torture, like burning of limbs, trampling to death by elephants and bulls, mutilating bodies, etc. Manu advocated for using torture to protect the society from the hands of the criminals. In Islamic administration stoning the adulterer, and other cruel forms of tortures, were in vogue.

Every human being is entitled to certain natural rights by virtue of his being a member of human society. The right to life, liberty and security of the citizens have been protected and the Constitution of India is one, which has rendered proper thought over these essential components. The right against subjection to torture, cruel treatment, inhuman behaviour or mental degradation are covered under natural justice system. The Human Rights organizations are much vocal about all these mal and malice treatments. In fact it has created terrible scare in the mind of the citizens. Activities of few desperate policemen have jeopardized the purity, sanctity and brevity of our constitution. The police should be people's police — trusted, respected and admired by the public. People must be free from fear or tyranny. Police is the visible symbol of authority of the government. In democracy each functionary of the government is ultimately accountable to the people. In fact, the term "torture", as such, has been referred and defined only in three instruments viz, the International

Declaration of Torture (1975), the Convention on Torture and other Cruel Treatments (1984) and the International Convention on the Suppression and Punishment of the Crime of Apartheid (1973).

According to Art 41 of the Convention against Torture and other Cruel, Inhuman or Degrading Treatment or Punishment, Torture means and includes:

(a) Intentional infliction of severe pain or suffering, whether physically or mentally upon a person.

(b) Which are primarily caused to obtain information or a confession, by way of intimidating or coercing, to ascertain the veracity of the charge or suspicion laid on him, which are illegal steps to cause pain or suffering toeing investigation to inflict punishment. Torture is thus an aggravated and deliberate form of treatment or cruelty and also an offence to malign human dignity.

The Universal Declaration of Human Rights, in it's Art 5, writes, "No one shall be subjected to torture, cruel, inhuman or degrading treatment or punishment." It has paid much attention to tortures meted on the children too (Art 37). It has further made the State a party and advocated for proper implementation of the resolutions. The United Nations General Assembly adopted a Code of Conduct for law enforcement officials on 17 December, 1976 wherein TORTURE has been defined "as any act by which severe pain or suffering, whether physical or mental, is intentionally inflicted by or at the instigation of public official on a person for such purposes as obtained from him or a third person information or confession, punishing him for an act he has committed, or intimidating him or other persons. It does not include pain or suffering arising only from, inherent in or incidental, to lawful sanctions to the extent consistent with the Standard Minimum Rules for the treatment of Prisoners."

Fake encounters are other brutal methods of elimination, whether genuine or fake. Rape in police custody or outraging the modesty of the women at the police station are also not uncommon. Another kind of events sparking sensitivity are using of police to inflict tortures upon political opponents by the government in power.

Third degree can be said to be the cruel and inhuman method of extracting information from the criminals. The concept of "Third Degree" derives its origin from Free Masonry, an institution of the skilled stone workers of the middle ages in Europe. 33 degrees have been listed in Free Masonry. In 1910 Major Richard, the then President of the Association of Chiefs of Police in the USA, coined the phrase "Third Degree" into police parlance to denote the physical force used on a suspect by the police, in custody. This concept of the third degree is the most iniquitous, nefarious, barbarous, heinous, villainous, atrocious and diabolical act committed by the State and as such is also termed as State terrorism. It is a hydra headed monster, which is eroding the faith of the people against the police system. It is not only tarnishing the image and reputation of the police, but also distancing and alienating the police from the mainstream of the welfare state mechanism. People, by and large, became allergic and have lost trust and faith upon the police. The symptom is a dangerous trend, which requires to be addressed. Indian Constitution has also laid due consideration to protect and safeguard the citizens from these atrocious actions. The Apex Court of India added phenomenal pressure on the State and the administration, which could be assessed by studying few landmark judgements, which has been discussed in depth in next chapter.

Few conditions lawfully endorsed, are enumerated below :

A person is considered to be innocent till his guilt is proved. He cannot be compelled to testify against his own guilt. His arrest must be made known. He should be produced before a magistrate within 24 hours of his arrest minus the journey period. He is entitled to have legal support and his police custody starts as soon as he is apprehended. In other words, the Police is responsible for what all happened after the apprehension and arrest is no more a secret affair. In spite of all the restrictions and bindings, the worst violation of human rights take place during the course of investigation, of which interrogation is also a part. In order to extract truth or to break the subject the technique applied by the investigators is "third degree" or torture. This violation of the Rule of Law has been controlled but not yet been abolished in spite of many punitive actions initiated against the erring officials.

The National Human Rights Commission (NHRC) under the Chairpersonship of Mr. Justice MN Venkatchaliah urged the Government of India to honour the obligations of the International Covenant of Civil and Political Rights and the Rights against Torture has been judicially recognized by the Supreme Court as a Fundamental Right and also obligated the States to recognize and implement the same. Failure to comply the prescribed requirements shall render liable for contempt of court.

Sec. 24 of the Indian Evidence Act has clearly stated that a confession made by an accused person is irrelevant in a criminal proceeding, if the making of the confession appears to the Court to have been caused by any inducement, threat or promise, having reference to the charge against the accused person, proceeding from a person in authority and sufficient, in the opinion of the Court, to give the accused person grounds which would appear to him reasonable, for supporting that by making it he would gain any advantage or avoid any evil of a temporal nature in reference to the proceedings against him. Sec. 25 of the Indian Evidence Act further imposed restrictions as this section goes in recording, "No confession made to a police officer shall be proved as against a person accused of any offence". The object of this particular section is to ensure that the person accused of the offence is not induced by threat, coercion or force to make a confessional statement [Anirudh Singh v. State AIR 1997 S C 2480] Sec. 330 of the Indian Penal Code prescribed punishment with imprisonment of either description for a term which may extend to seven years, and also be liable to fine in case of voluntarily causing hurt to seven years, and also be liable to fine in case of voluntarily causing hurt to extort confession or to compel restoration of property. Sec. 331 further enhanced punishment to ten years in case of voluntarily causing grievous hurt to extort confession, or to compel restoration of property. Sec. 163 CrPC states that no police officer or other person in authority shall offer or make, or cause to be offered or made, any such inducement, threat or promise as is mentioned in Sec. 24 of the Indian Evidence Act, 1872.

Force and degree of the application of the force, remain still a confusing state. The police are permitted to use force but there are restrained provisions and limitations. The force is used by the police during arrests, search, crowd control, unlawful assembly dispersement and even on self-protection or defence. The limitations of the use depend on the situational demand and threat perceptions. Section 46 CrPC empowers police to use all means of necessary measures to effect arrest. The word "necessary" is not cleared even U/S Sec. 49 CrPC. Sec.129 CrPC empowers the Executive Magistrate and the Police Officer above the rank of SI to use force to disperse any unlawful assembly in order to contain law and order related disturbances. Here also the word "minimum" level of using force has been the core-confusing component. Similarly, a private person can also use force, subject to restrictions, in exercise of his right of private defence (Sec S96-106 IPC).

The fundamental principles of criminal jurisprudence provides burden of proof on the prosecution, that to beyond reasonable doubt and any benefit of doubt must go in favour of the accused. The Supreme Court also laid down legal dicta that the accused in pre-trial detention is entitled to fair and decent treatment by way of comforts, medical attention, etc. "The Police, with their wide powers are apt to overstep their zeal to detect crimes, and are tempted to use the strong arm against those who happen to fall under their secluded jurisdiction. That tendency and that temptations must in the larger interest of justice, be nipped in the bud" [1977 SEC.-Cr.- PP-444-445].

Third degree is a very sensitive topic, which has even sparked the society. The Human Rights Organizations and alike bodies have kept this aspect under close observation and in case of any reported violation they are much vocal. The Bhagalpur blinding case (Khatri v. State of Bihar AIR 1981 Sc. 928) and the brutal torture and murder of Thangjam Manorama @ Henthoi, a 32 years old woman, by 17 BN. Assam Rifles in Manipur (August, 2004) are alarming instances.

REASONS HIGHLIGHTED

The main reason for the growth of torture is the over zealousness of the investigating officer to secure conviction since conviction is considered as the yardstick of latter's professional competency.

The reasons behind this gruesome method may be :

1. Easy and quick method to subjugate an interrogee.
2. Quick orientation of results.
3. Increased workload of the police. Practically less rest period.
4. Paucity of time.
5. Positive result orientation ratio is higher by adopting third degree.
6. Lack of knowledge on tradecraft and criminology.
7. Official pressure for quick result orientation.
8. To extract money.
9. Lack of scientific and electronic gadgets and their handling capabilities.
10. Saddist attitude of the Police and Security Forces.
11. Political vendata and
12. Inadequate knowledge about recent court judgements, circulars, etc.

Amnesty International has recommended the following ten steps to halt torture practice and to create an effective institutional framework :

The government should publicly acknowledge that torture is used as a routine method of interrogation and intimidation in police stations and other places of detention. It should make the combat of torture an issue of high priority to which the entire nation should be committed. All political parties should adopt such a policy and implement it in the states where they are in power.

Judicial inquiries should be made mandatory into all allegations of torture, including rape and deaths in custody.

Witness should be protected from intimidation and harassment and those accused of torture suspended from duty during such inquiries. The inquiries should be conducted within a reasonable time and the results should immediately be made public. Special care should be taken to protect poor and illiterate victims who lack access to existing redress mechanisms. All detenues should have the right to a medical examination promptly after admission to the place of custody and regularly thereafter, and to be examined by a doctor whoever possible, are of crucial importance to women who allege they have been raped.

All the perpetrators should be brought to justice. Any abuses or violations of the directives invariably be accountable. That torture is forbidden must be well circulated. Victims, their legal representatives and their relatives who wish to prosecute police officials for criminal offences and/or sue for compensation should have a legally protected right of access to all relevant documentary evidence including police and other official records including post mortem reports.

The government should ensure that existing legal safeguards are respected under all circumstances, notably the rules that all detainees be produced before a magistrate within 24 hours of arrest and that women and children are not taken to police stations for purpose of investigation. The latter rule should be extended to include other places of interrogation such as army camps. The police should be given strict instructions to keep up-to-date centrally maintained registers of arrests and to promptly inform relatives of an arrest and the detainee's transfer. Access to relatives and lawyers should be prompt. Families of those who die in police custody should have the right to insist that a medical or other qualified person nominated by the family is present at the post-mortem. The government should draw up detailed guidelines for the interrogation of suspects and publish them after consulting with lawyers, bar associations, civil liberties groups and medical professional group. The government should allow independent bodies to regularly inspect all places where detainees are held. It should also allow the International Committee of the Red Cross (ICRC) access to all areas where there is armed conflict between the SFs and the opposition groups, notably J&K, Punjab, and North Eastern States.

A list of the rights of all detainees, in local language, should be displayed in all police cells and other such places and the detainees must be formally notified of their rights. The duties of the police under Sec. 29 of the Indian Police Act, not to perpetrate unwarrantable personal violence on persons in their custody and to ensure that they are safely kept, should be similarly displayed.

The government should institute an intensive programme of human rights education as a standard part of the training curriculum for all police, SFs personnel involved in the arrest, detention, and interrogation of suspects. International standard in this respect be followed. They should instruct all law enforcement personnels that orders from a superior officers are no defence against charges of torture. The government should undertake an urgent programme of police reform, so as to create a force free from political influence and patronage. It should review and improve the conditions of service of the police as well as their rights to organize and express themselves.

There should be a statutory rights to compensation. The Government should establish special tribunals solely charged with the allocation of prompt and adequate compensation to all victims of human rights violations. It should be paid by the appropriate state government or, in case of Army, the central government.

Appropriate facilities should be created in all Indian states for the medical treatment and rehabilitation of victims of torture and cruel, inhuman and degrading treatment.

The government should order an authoritative investigation into the causes and the pattern of torture in India and circumstances facilitating its widespread occurrence. These could be independent bodies in the various states formed to monitor such complaints and supervise appropriate follow up. At the national level, an ombudsman or multi-party legislative committee could be established with the staff and facilities to investigate patterns of torture and custodial deaths and ensure their prompt and effective investigation and follow up.

The government should strengthen its international commitment to prevent torture which it affirmed when it initiated and made a Unilateral Declaration against Torture in 1979. The government should respond in substance to the queries addressed to it by the UN Special Rapporteur on torture and UN Special Rapporteur on summary or arbitrary executions.

Relevant national and international bodies should be permitted free access to investigate reported human rights violations.

It is evident that torture or third degree method is a matter of agony before the authorities. Not only national pressure but also international thrust to end this malice practice have caused terrible vibration as India is a signatory (October, 1997) to the Convention Against Torture. India's image and position before the world body is at stake. The state sponsored terrorism can never be supported. The state should adhere other measures to counter terrorists, militants, and alike threats. The government and legislature must give serious thought about the recommendations made not only by the Apex Court but by other Commissions as well. In any case the protectors can never be law violators. India has a standing in the international forums, this aspect too should be kept in view. Iron handling of the offenders, proper motivation and effective training are recommended few options.

5 Legality of Interrogations

As a law enforcing officer, the duty of the police is to serve mankind, to protect lives and properties, to protect innocents, to maintain peace and tranquility, to respect the Constitution of India and also to curb crimes and book the law breakers. The police is also symbolic of public faith, trust and dedicated to the cause of the society. The entire process of interrogation is based on the principle of Natural Justice. Both the interrogator and the interrogee are fastened with certain legal bindings and liable for punishment for violation of laws and also negligence towards suspect who is put to interrogation. He is not a prisoner till he is convicted by the legal institution and therefore he enjoys all rights and privileges. None can be compelled to plead guilty in any crime. Everyone has a right to silence.

Interrogation is a process of investigation by a legally empowered authority and to elicit the truth. It can never be viewed that since a person is put to interrogation his complicity is there. Thus an interrogator should be an unbiased mind person who is vowed to elicit the truth only. As a true professional he should adhere to this ethics. The faultline lies when the interrogator becomes prejudice and overestimates himself, which ultimately put him to embarrassment and also malign the popular image of his organization before the society. The treatment, handling and tackling varies subject wise and nationality wise. Indians are governed by Indian Laws, which may not be a compelling factor for foreign nationals who are often subjected to their national laws, various International Conventions and Statutes. Care and cautions must be paid upon different judgements pronounced by the Courts in restricting, modifying and repealing legal bindings. Thus a professional interrogator must have thorough knowledge of both laws of the land as well as of international laws. As for example, both the foreign diplomats and non-diplomatic cadre staff members posted in their Missions in India enjoy immunity under the Geneva Convention and they can maximum be made persona-non-grata if their activities are found prejudicial to the interest of our nation. While the agents employed by them, who are being Indians, are charged in accordance to Indian Laws.

The concept of the rights of human beings is neither western nor modern. *Rig Veda, Mahabharata* and even *Arthasastra* spoke of individual freedom and liberties. Promulgation of the Constitution of India on November 26, 1949 which came into effect in January, 1950, not only enshrined protection of fundamental rights but also laid emphasis on social justice system. As in Human Rights, the emphasis is on basic human dignity, the basic principle that an individual is presumed to be innocent till the contrary is proved against him which has been enshrined in Article 21 of Indian Constitution and Art 14(2) of the International Covenant of Civil and Political Rights, 1960. Indian Human Rights Act, 1993 defined Human Rights as "the rights relating to liberty, equality and dignity of the individual guaranteed by the Indian Constitution as embodied in the Fundamental Rights and the International Covenants".

The Supreme Court of India has referred to the International Covenants while dealing with Human Rights violations. For example, in the Prem Shankar Case (AIR 1980 S.C. 1535) the Supreme Court, while dealing with handcuffs and other humiliations in custody, observed, "After all, even while discussing the relevant statutory provisions and constitutional requirements, court and counsel must never forget the core principle found in Article 5 of the Universal Declaration of Human Rights, 1948. No one shall be subjected to torture or to cruel, inhuman or degrading treatment or punishment". Similarly, the Court vide State of Maharashtra v. Ravikant S. Patil (1991-2 SEC-373) held handcuffing and parading of under-trial prisoner contravening to Art. 21 of the Indian Constitution.

Every law enforcing official, which includes the interrogator, is a part of Criminal Justice System, which aims to detect, deter and destroy crime and also to upheld the whole system securing people's respect. Gone are the days, of "eye for eye", "tooth for tooth". Use of strong arm or third degree concept has got no place in interrogation. The Code of Conduct for Police adopted in 1985 by the Government of India has prescribed norms, restrictions, behaviour pattern and controls. Since Indian law is very clear about the treatments which may be meted to the interrogee, it remained bounden duty of the interrogators to follow the guidelines and orders.

Indian law, being a true democratic set up and a welfare state always paid proper focus on justice and justice only. Benefit of reasonable doubt goes to the accused. This principle is based on the ground and consideration that no innocent person be subjected to punishment, unless his guilt, involvement or complicity is proved beyond doubt. The evidentiary position must conform the guilt and no hypothesis or probability be taken into consideration. Therefore the role of the interrogators in collecting convincing evidences and proof to justify the crime committed and the part played by each perpetrators. "It is not the quantity of evidence but the quality that weighs with the court" (State v. Rambali & Others, 1953 CrLJ 428 All). The court cannot convict on a finding of mere conjuncture or probability (Sheo Mani Shaw v. State 1953 CrLJ 1399). At the same time, it is a fact that the accused is entitled to have the benefit of only reasonable doubt not to every doubt, hunch or hesitancy. Therefore, this legal aspect should invariably be kept in mind by the interrogators, while on the assignment and they should concentrate on collecting concrete, reasonable and convincing evidences which the judiciary would accept.

The prosecution must prove both the *actus reus* and the *mens rea* beyond reasonable doubt. Largely giving the accused the benefit of doubt, Indian Court rely heavily on the testimony of witnesses. Sec 163 CrPC prevents police using inducement and threats to get confessions. Confession is a direct acknowledgement of the guilt. Admission is the statement of the accused, direct or implied, of facts, pertinent to the issue, and tending, in connection with proof of other facts, to prove the guilt, but of itself insufficient to authorize a conviction.

The stringent attitude on the part of the authorities has been regarded as a very sensitive and articulated step. In order to avert torture, the interrogees put forward convincing truth which under court's scanner are proved as false and fabricated. Pressure mounted on the interrogators have forced them to evolve new techniques and they have now reformed and educated themselves. It is not be muscle but the brain became the instrument of success. More research and studies are on. Both the organization as well as the components i.e. the officers are much serious in their endeavour.

PROVISIONS OF LAW

The provisions of law governing interrogations are discussed below in brief :

The Constitutional provisions are :

Art. 20(1) : No person shall be convicted of any offence except for violation of law in force at the time of the commission of the act charged as an offence, nor be subjected to a penalty greater than which might have been inflicted under the law in force at the time of the commission of the offence.

Art. 20(3) : No person accused of any offence shall be compelled to be a witness against himself..

Art. 22(1) : No person who is arrested shall be detained in custody without being informed, as soon as may be, of the grounds for such arrest nor shall be denied the right to consult, and to be defended by a legal practitioner of his choice.

Art. 22 (2) : Every person who is arrested and detained in custody shall be produced before the nearest magistrate within a period of twenty four hours of such arrest excluding the time necessary for the journey from the place of arrest to the court of the magistrate and no such person shall be detained in custody beyond the said period without the authority of a magistrate.

Art. 22(3) : Nothing in clauses (1) and (2) shall apply —

a) To any person who for the time being is an enemy alien, or

b) To any person who is arrested or detained under any law providing for preventive detention.

Code of Criminal Procedure, 1973

Some relevant sections though not having direct bearing on interrogation but discussed for awareness.

Sec. 160 : - Examination of Witnesses

1) Any police officer making an investigation under this chapter may, by order in writing, require the attendance before himself of any person being within the limits of his own or any adjoining station who, from the information given, or otherwise, appears to be acquainted with the facts and circumstances of the case, and such person shall attend as so required :

   Provided that no male person or woman under the age of fifteen years shall be required to attend at any place other than the place in which such male person or woman resides.

2) The State Government may, by rules made itself, provide for the payment by the police officer of the reasonable expenses of every person attending under sub-section (1) at any place other than his residence.

Sec. 161 : Examination of witness by police :

1) Any police officer making an investigation under this chapter, or any police officer not below such rank as the State Government may, by general or special order, prescribe in this behalf, acting on the requisition of such officer, be acquainted with the facts and circumstance of the case.

2) Such person shall be bound to answer truly all questions relating to such case put to him such officer, other than questions the answers to which would have a tendency to expose him to a criminal charge or to a penalty or forfeiture.

3) The police officer may reduce into writing any statement made to him in the course of an examination under this section, and if he does so, he shall make a separate and true record of the statement of each such person whose statement he records.

Sec. 162: Statements to police not to be signed : Use of statements in evidence :

1) No statements made by any person to a police officer in the course of an investigation under this chapter shall, if reduced to writing, be signed by the person making it, nor shall any such statement or record, thereof, whether in a police diary or otherwise or any part of such statement or record, be used for any purpose, save as hereinafter provided, at any inquiry or trial in respect of any offence under investigation at the time when such statement was made.

   Provided that when any witness is called for the prosecution in such inquiry or trial whose statement has been reduced into writing as aforesaid, any part of his statement, if duly proved, may be used by the accused, and with the permission of the Court, by the prosecution, to contradict such witness in the manner provided by section 145 of the Indian Evidence Act, 1872 (1 of 1872), and when any part of such statement is so used, any part thereof may also be used in the reexamination of such witness, but for the purpose only of explaining any matter referred to in his cross-examination.

2) Nothing in this section shall be deemed to apply to any statement falling within the provisions of clause (1) of section 32 of the Indian Evidence Act, 1872 (1 of 1872) or to affect the provisions of section 27 of that Act.

Explanation : An omission to state a fact or circumstance in the statement referred to in sub-section(1) may amount to contradiction if the same appears to be significant and otherwise relevant having regard to the context in which such omission occurs and whether any omission amount to a contradiction in the particular context shall be a question of fact.

Sec 57 : Persons arrested not to be detained more than twenty four hours :

No police officer shall detain in custody a person arrested without warrant for a longer period than under all the circumstances of the case is reasonable, and such period shall not in absence of a special order of a Magistrate under section 167, exceed twenty four hours exclusive of the time necessary for the journey from the place of arrest to the Magistrate court.

Indian Penal Code Provisions

Sec. 330 : Voluntarily causing hurt to extort confession, or to compel restoration of property.

Whoever voluntarily causes hurt for the purpose of extorting from the sufferer or from any person interested in the sufferer, any confession or any information which may lead to the detection of any offence or misconduct, or for the purpose of constraining the sufferer or any person interested in the sufferer to restore or to cause the restoration of any property of valuable security or to satisfy any claim or demand, or to give information which may to the restoration of any property or valuable security, shall be punished with imprisonment of either description for a term which may extend to seven years, and shall also be liable to fine.

[Case Ref : Sham Kant v. State. 1992 CrLJ 3243 SC]

i) The police officer tortures one for confession.

ii) The police officer tortures one to induce him to point out where certain stolen property is deposited.

iii) A Revenue Officer tortures one to compel him to pay certain due arrears of revenue.

Sec. 331 : Voluntarily causing grievous hurt to extort confession, or to compel restoration of property.

Whoever voluntarily causes grievous hurt for the purpose of extorting from the sufferer, or from any person interested in the sufferer, any confession or any information which may lead to the detection of an offence or misconduct, or for the purpose of constraining the sufferer to restore or to cause the restoration of any property or valuable security, or to satisfy any claim or demand, or to give information which may lead to the restoration of any property or valuable security, shall be punished with imprisonment of either description for a term which may extend to ten years, and shall also be liable to fine.

Sec. 348 : Wrongful confinement to extort confession or compel restoration of property.

Whoever wrongfully confines any person for the purpose of extorting from the person confined or any person interested in the person confined any confession or any information which may lead to the detection of an offence or misconduct, or for the purpose of constraining the person confined or any person interested in the person confined to restore or to cause the restoration of any property or valuable security or to satisfy any claim or demand, or to give information which may lead to the restoration of any property or valuable security, shall be punished with imprisonment of either description for a term which may extend to three years, and shall also be liable to fine.

Conditions apply :

i) Causing grievous hurt.

ii) Voluntarily caused.

iii) To extort confession, detection.

iv) To specify the claim, or degree and

v) Restoration of property.

Indian Evidence Act, 1872 Provisions

Sec. 24 : Confession caused by inducement, threat or promise, when irrelevant in criminal proceeding.

A confession made by an accused person is irrelevant in a criminal proceeding, if the making of the confession appears to the Court to have been caused by any inducement, threat or promise, having reference to the charge against the accused person grounds which would appear to him reasonable, for supposing that by making it he would gain any advantage or avoid any evil of a temporal nature in reference to the proceedings against him.

Sec. 25 : Confession to police officer not to be proved.

No confession made to a police officer shall be proved as against a person accused of any offence.

Sec. 26 : Confession by accused while in custody of police not to be proved against him.

No confession made by a person whilst he is in the custody of a police officer, unless it be made in the immediate presence of Magistrate, shall be proved as against such person.

Sec. 27 : How much information received from accused may be proved.

Provided that, when any fact is deposed to as discovered in consequences of information received from a person accused of any offence in the custody of a police officer, so much of such information, whether it amounts to a confession or not, as relates distinctly to the fact thereby discovered, may be proved.

The Official Secret Act, 1923 Provision : Sec. 8

Duty of giving information as to the commission of offences :

It shall be the duty of every person to give on demand to a SP, or other police officer not below the rank of Inspector, empowered by an IG or CP in this behalf, or to any member of the Armed Forces of the Union engaged on guard, sentry, patrol or other similar duty, any information in his power relating to an offence or suspected offence under Sec.3 or under Sec.3 read with Sec.9 and if so required, and upon tender of his reasonable expenses, to attend at such reasonable time and place as may be specified for the purpose of furnishing such information.

There are few special laws and acts also dealing with the subject. These provisions also need to be studied and acted upon.

SPECIAL PROVISION FOR WOMEN

In spite of the tall claims made by the feminist bodies and few Civil Rights organizations about the status and position of the women in India, their unequal position is still a matter of debate. While conducting interrogation of the women subjects few cautionary notes emanate. The Constitution of India vide Art. 14 has guaranteed equality before the law and equal protection of laws while Art. 15(1) has restrained the State not to discriminate on the ground of sex. Art. 16(1) further provide equal employment opportunity. Art. 51(A) protect the dignity of the women. Constitution has paid due attention to women and further ensured their protection, equality, job opportunity and dignity. Indian laws specially the IPC, CrPC, the Child Marriage Restraint Act, the Immoral Traffic (Prevention) Act, the Dowry Prohibition Act, the Indecent Representation of Women (Prohibition) Act, Commission of Sati (Prevention) Act, the Family Courts Act, Maternity Benefit Act, Equal Remuneration Act and the Special Marriage Act have further consolidated the position and status of the women.

The National Human Rights Commission (NHRC) in its annual report (1994-95) mentioned, "Though the UN Convention on Elimination of all Forms of Discrimination Against Women (CEDAW) was adopted in the General Assembly in 1979, India rectified it in June, 1993. The provisions of the CEDAW would now have to be implemented by way of internal laws and administrative regulations. The Commission recommends vigorous implementation of the country's obligation under this Convention." In India specially in the villages, majority of the women still observe purdah. Besides social stigma, economic condition, poor education, lack of proper cultural development, etc. are matters which have direct reflexion on interrogation. The position of the girls in our society and the concern of the parents to safeguard and protect chastity and character of their wards specifically force to hide even the crime. The moral courage upliftment, social activists and NGOs propaganda and care, a high degree of decorum and decency projected by the interrogators and ruthless actions against the offenders are few points which may encourage the victims to fight against the perpetrators. While interrogating a female, specially, the victim enormous amount of patience is required. Services of the women police should be requisitioned. In case of non-availability of women police, an elderly woman of the locality be placed to interrogate and preferably in presence of a relative of the subject. In fact, every considerable allowance, as per requirement, should be made to female witness. Testimony of a woman is equal to that of a man. Hence, while interrogating a woman equal importance is required to be paid.

6 Aids to Interrogation

The search for effective aids to interrogation is probably as old as the human urge to extract truth mainly from deceitful subjects. With the passage of time and bestowed on continuous research, experiment and harping, few human, chemical and scientific tools have emerged useful and gained place in the process of interrogations which are termed as the "aids to interrogation." These tools, barring the human one, are the result of scientific and technological developments. These are also known as NARCO Analysis Test or Truth Serum Test in Forensic Science. These tools have substituted painstaking and time-consuming efforts of the Crime Investigators and have also replaced use of third degree method, which is now totally "banned" under the law. These aids are comparatively new in the annals of police investigation and still lack total legal acceptability. Law is a living process, which changes according to evolution and development of society, science, ethics and so on. The criminal justice system should be based on just, equitable and reasoning principles. The gradual acceptance of these aids have marked a significant role in evidence collection process, and have also enhanced the scope and utility to further interrogation. Exploitation of physical, psychological, ethical and mental conditions is a technique commonly used by expert interrogators to ascertain the "truth", "falsehood", "lie", "deception", etc. Body and mind languages could easily be read with the help of few scientific gadgets and by administering few recognized serums/drugs. Reading of one's mind and gaining proximity and confidence is also made easy. No court ruling or legislation would aim to make police work more complicated.

Police is also an instrument who not only fixes the criminal but also brings the culprit to book by way of collecting legal evidence. Therefore, the up-comingness in the interrogation and continuous search or thrive for finding out new ways and means are welcome in this electronic age.

OBJECTIVES AND SCOPE

1. Aids to interrogation have been gaining gradual importance owing to effectiveness and generation of positive results.
2. Search for effective aids to interrogation would continue so long deceptiveness of the interrogees would exist.
3. Neo modus operandi and increase of sophisticated crimes would put pressure to evolve new counter-measure and techniques. Science and Technology are not static in components.
4. These tools have eased the mental pressure of the interrogators and also minimised time span.
5. These mechanisms are mainly harping on the mind and body (psyche and physique) of the subject. Hence debarred from the so-called torture orientation.
6. The involvement of the courts, experts and psychologists have lessened the burden of the interrogators.
7. The prognosis or the report may be corroborated with other evidences.
8. The pressure is mounted on the subject over his consciousness, reasoning power, memory and resistance.
9. Human Rights activists have already termed these actions as "psychological third degree".
10. Section 45 of the Indian Evidence Act is silent on forensic tests like Narco-analysis etc.

CATEGORISED

HUMAN AND SCIENCE AIDS TO INTERROGATION

AIDS

HUMAN

1. STOOL PIGEON
2. FAKE DOCTOR

CHEMICAL

NARCOANALYSIS
OR
TRUTH SERUM TEST

SCOPOLAMINE
CHLOROFORM
MORPHINE
PENOBARBITAL
SECONAL
SODIUM PENTOTHAL

SCIENTIFIC

POLYGRAPH
P-300 (BRAIN MAPPING)
C.C.T.V
TWO-WAY MIRROR
SENSITIVE CAMERA
PSYCHOLOGICAL STRESS
EVATUATOR
MARK 2 VOICE ANALYSER

HUMAN AIDS

In this process a human being is planted in the lockup of the subject, with a view to extracting truth from the deceptive suspect by gaining his confidence. The interlocutor is selected very carefully, trained and then launched as undercover. He is properly briefed about the case and the subject and must live with his cover. Both his launching and retrieval should be done in a very careful way not to arose any suspicion or doubt. Both these two human aids, described hereunder, are time tested and widely accepted techniques used by the interrogators to broach silence of the subject.

Nevertheless, these two human aids have got no legal sanction but the information gained through these techniques tremendously help in breaking the subject. Video and audio recordings are advisable as these can be displayed if needed. Acting ability of the interlocutors is the key factor. This theory is based on the principle of association and mutual trust.

Stool Pigeon System

A very old method widely used in criminal investigation. A very popular and effective technique used in interrogation too. Placing a trained person in the cover of a criminal in the lockup or the place where the interrogee is kept, with the purpose to befriend the subject and tactfully extract the truth, is the technique. It remained a fact that during the course of interrogation, the subject often maintains alertness, which he loosens when he retries at his place. His conviction and deceptiveness gets defused as soon as he is off from the clutches of the interrogation. He feels a sigh of relief for the time being. A known and won criminal or even an unknown policeman may be carefully selected, trained and properly briefed. Prior to his physical launching appearance, dress, and other modes must match as per situational requirements. His body must bear signs of physical tortures, even blood stains. His acting ability and behaviour like a criminal are core points.

He should refrain from immediate interaction with the subject, he must adopt gradual stepping. Gradually he builds his rapport with the subject by sharing family scores and blaming his luck, etc. In this process he develops his intimacy with the subject to share feelings and the "undisclosed portion" of which the interrogators may be interested. This system is also a psychological game wherein the "right in place situation" is created and the mental barriers are broken. Many a times, MCR is provided for recording the conversation and the "stool pigeon" taking plea of urinal may change or hand over the cassette to the interrogator or his agent, obviously avoiding the notice of the interrogee. Retrieval of the stool pigeon is also done very carefully.

This system may also be very useful in jails where both convicted and undertrial criminals are lodged. In jails, the criminals feel free and openness. They also develop fellow feelings and often receive guidance and assistances from hardened criminals. Jails now-a-days, have become a hatchery of hard criminals and militants. Stool pigeon plantation may produce effective result in crime investigation and crime intelligence generations. The potentiality of Stool Pigeon will depend upon his living with the cover and withstanding capability.

Fake Doctor

Doctors have got very significant position in our society. Human beings are subjected to various kinds of diseases and deformities. None is desirous to die. People are mostly faithful, truthful, loyal and obedient to the doctors. Respect them obviously to lead a comfortable and painless life. Doctors are also respected by the criminals and former's services are often requisitioned by them. The criminal-doctors relations is not a new one. Still the touchy and human behaviour, together with sympathetic approach of the doctor, subjugate any criminal. The system is launching of a person under the cover of a doctor and thereby gather the truth from the interrogee. The person selected must be trained and he must have the knowledge and prudency of a doctor. He must have know-how of a doctor. He must be equipped with the medical kits and his dress must be in conformity with a doctor. By way of checking, examination and treatment he not only develops rapport but also creates a place in the mind of the subject. In this process, he breaks the subject and extract the "concealed information." Doctors often adopt a technique that the subject should release his tension otherwise the blood pressure would further shoot up, which may produce mental stress, rapidly increasing palpitations, heart convulsion and thereby make him to disclose the truth. The fake doctors must practice his cover prior to his launching. He should also visit and examine other criminals in the same premises to consolidate his cover. Prior to launching a "fake doctor" in jail, utter secrecy may be maintained and the concerned jailor may be taken into confidence.

CHEMICAL AIDS

Chemical aids to interrogation are known as Narco Analysis Test or Truth Serum Test.

Scientists, specially neurologists, have made several experiments with a variety of narcotic/sedative/anesthetic/intoxicant/drugs on human body to observe biological effect. It is believed that if a person is administered a specific drug which suppresses his reasoning power without affecting his memory and speech, he can be made to tell the truth. These drugs affect central nervous system and bring the individual to a semi-conscious state. The individual looses his self-control, deceptive imagination and is unable to manipulate answers. Answers often be spontaneous and void of any "well thought of" or concoction. The entire idea is to dull subject's consciousness to a degree and to diminish his will-power. Caution must be taken to limit the dose so that the memory and consciousness remain intact. In fact, as a matter of rule these drugs are administrated under Court's order, in a government hospital by authorized medical practitioner and with the consent of the subject. Doze and periodicities are determined after examination of the subject's physical condition, mental state, etc. Wrong doze can send him to coma and even to death. In the case of an abuser of other intoxicant/narcotic, the truth serum may not evolve any impact on him. The subject cleverly dodge the examiner pretending to be in semi-conscious state and tell lies. Thus during the process of physical examination proper attention is warranted. All revelations made under the influence of truth serum drugs may not be always correct. As these are made under the suffering influence of the drugs administrated are not freely revealed. The effect of bio-molecules on the bio-activity of an individual is evident as the drugs tolled upon the central nervous system, lowers blood pressure and slows heart beating rate. The individual is put into a hypnotic state and is deprived of normal and natural inhibition. In other words, he remains in a "twilight state." In this context it may be kept in mind that these truth serums i.e. narco analysis test drugs are also prescribed by the psychiatrists for the treatment of mentally ill or disordered patients.

In India a special Court dealing with cases under the Maharashtra Control of Organized Crimes Act (MCOCA) in Pune allowed the Special Investigation Team (SIT) probling Telgi Fake Stamp Paper case accused Abdul Karim Telgi to undergo Polygraph test, P-300 or Brain Mapping Test, and Narco analysis Test at Karnataka Forensic Science Laboratory, Bangalore on Dec. 20-22, 2003 to facilitate the investigation. The defence lawyers and the Human Rights bodies contested this order and pointed that narco analysis test was in a very primitive form of investigation and the report obtained had no evidential value owing to violation of Art 20(3) of the Constitution of India.

The Bombay High Court in a landmark verdict in the case of Ramchandra Reddy v. State of Maharashtra (2004 All MR - CR - 1740) upheld the legality of the use of P-300, Polygraph and Narco analysis tests. The Court allowed the SIT to conduct these scientific tests on the accused of the Telgi case including Abdul Karim Telgi. A distinction was drawn between "statement" (made before a police officer) and "testimony" (made under oath in Court). Justice Palshikar and Justice Kakade observed that lie-detector and brain mapping tests did not involve any statement being made and the statement made under narco analysis was not admissible in evidence during trial. The judgement also held that these tests involve "minimal bodily harm". Court also put Abu Salem in similar tests at the Karnataka Forensic Science Laboratory.

Narco analysis tests, as tools of interrogation considered to be less hazardous as compared to third degree treatments. Though the H.R. groups coined this test as "psychological third degree". They also highlighted the abrasion of the highly acknowledged maxim "*Nemo Tenetur Se Ipsum Accusare*" (No man, not even the accused himself can be compelled to answer any question, which may tend to prove him guilty of a crime, he has been accused of).

In spite of the merits of the tests, reliability and legal validity i.e. admissibility in courts of law are yet to be cleared. The criminal justice system is never a static process. It changes keeping informity with the changing crime scenario, modus operandi, advancement of science and technology, social changes and over all institutional need.

SCIENTIFIC AIDS

With the advancement of science and technology few new tools have come into prominence, which are used as tools of interrogation. Continuous research and development specially after the World War and the increasing demands finally marked the following few scientific tools or electronic gadgets, which for the purpose of interrogation are termed as scientific aids to interrogation. Though these items are in use but research and development process is still on. Handicap of these tools is that these require expert / professional handling and are yet to be totally legally accepted on evidential count. Moreover, the availability and use of some of these tools are restricted and limited. Advantage include lessening of painstaking and time consuming process and orientation of quick result. The outcry of the Human Rights and other such bodies highlighting adoption of third degree method has also been submerged and minimized after the introduction of these tools to a greater extent. Moreover, a fear psychosis has engulfed affecting the crime scenario too. Though the Indian laws have not legally accepted the validity in the light of legal principles, but in many judgements the Courts have acknowledged the results of these tests on count of legal testimony.

The scientific tools and aids are :

- Polygraph i.e. Lie Detector.
- Psychological Stress Evaluator.
- Mark 2 Voice Analyser.

- Two-Way Mirror.
- Bugging Devices.
- Micro Cassette Recorder.
- Sensitive Cameras and CCTV
- P-300 Or Brain Mapping.
- DNA Profiling.

POLYGRAPH

Polygraph, which is commonly known as "Lie Detector" is based on the principle that when an individual conceals or tempers some information in response to some question, notable physiological changes occur which are beyond the control of the person put on polygraph. The changes include pulse rate, blood pressure, skin resistance, and sweating. The Lie Detector merely records such physiological changes with regard to some crucial or non-crucial questions. It involves a diagnostic technique for interpreting, recording and evaluating the responses generated by the subject and recorded in the machine. The examination, conducted by the experts and not by the interrogators, is based on an assumption that there is an interaction between the mind and body and is conducted by various components or the sensors of a polygraph machine, which are attached to the body of the person who is interrogated. It is nevertheless the job of an expert. Incompetent persons would not be able to read and evaluate the readings.

Room : Lie detector test should be done in a quite and private room. There must not be any extraneous noise. Presence of arresting officers, interrogators, or any spectator should not be there. In this room there should not be any picture which can distract examinee's mind. The light and furniture arrangements too should be as per requirements. Excessive or glaring illumination should be avoided.

Process and Steps : The data obtained from polygraph are analysed and interpreted on the basis of certain recognized principles. Before the subject is put on lie detector test, he is thoroughly examined by a competent physician. After all the prescribed tests if he is found medically fit then only he is allowed to sit for the polygraph test. The experts then set the procedure and mode of test. The subject i.e. the examinee is also warned that the data obtained with the help of the instrument can be used against him. The pre-test interview is very important. If the examiner can prevail upon the examinee in right direction, many a time the examinee divulges the truth even before applying the test. It is a psychological pressure mounted on the examinee who remains in a confusing state of mind about the reality and scope of this test. The process is, the instrument is attached to subject and the questions are put to him to emanate answers. The instrument starts recording changes in breathing, blood pressure, sweat activity, skin resistance, etc. Framing of questions must be in such a fashion that should cause some emotional effects and disturbances in the mind of the examinee.

Questioning : The case study, studying the examinee, and various psychological bearings form components to frame, suitable questionnaire. There may be two parts of the questionnaire; one the crucial i.e. which has direct bearings with the case and the second is non-crucial i.e. those questions which have no or less bearing in the investigation. The role of the crucial questions, therefore, is much significant as these are connected with the guilt part. Innocence, connivance or involvement of the person who is under examination can be gauged by putting crucial questions and obtaining the physiological changes. Response to a critical question emanates specific response and helps the examiner to arrive at a conclusion either in favour of or against the subject. Proposition could be had from crucial question only. The experienced examiners put non-crucial questions at the very outset and then switched over to the crucial ones in order to ascertain specific responses which are much significant in this process. Moreover, it is wise to put several crucial questions instead of one, with a view to exhibiting reactions and changes, specially to identify innocence. In case of one crucial question, the examinee owing to nervousness may response positive.

Compositions : The latest polygraph machine is composed in three distinct units, namely :

Pheumograph

It is an electro-mechanical machine which is used for recording the changes in the rate of respiration of the subject at the time of interrogation. Pheumograph is a partially inflated rubber tube or a rubber tube around a flexible coil of wire and is fastened securely either across the chest or the abdominal region of the subject by means of a chain. It is connected by a rubber tube with a tambour and a recording pen. With the variations of pressure caused by respiratory process, the tambour moves through a lever system and causes the pen to make a tracing on the paper graph. In the case of a normal person, with a calm and balanced mind, the respiration and expiration are regular and rhythmical. But in the case of a guilty person whose mind remains agitated owing to the very desire to conceal or hide the truth i.e. his deceptiveness, the regularity and tranquility of respiration and expiration process is found to be disturbed. These changes are duly recorded with the help of this instrument and analysed by the experts. Usually regular respiration is observed before the test. Just prior to the lie, respiration gets restrained and thereafter breathing becomes deeper during the rest of the test.

Cardiosphymograph

It is an apparatus for recording the changes in the blood pressure and pulse rate of the examinee under scanner. Usually a rubber cuff is fastened snugly around the arm or the lower leg of the examinee or just above his ankle. The cuff is connected with the polygraph by means of a rubber tube end thus facilitates the mechanical recording of the blood pressure and pulse rate during the test. Generally an irregularity in the blood pressure is noticed upto the lie but the pressure increases to the highest peak at the point of lie. Slowing of the pulse beat just after a reply and a sharp fall in the blood pressure several seconds after the reply are indicative of deception. The changes in the systolic blood pressure and pulse rate are recorded in a recorder.

Phycho-Galvanograph

It is an instrument for recording changes in skin resistance, which is also known as electro-dermal response. The emotional disturbances like the fear, uneasiness, tension and worriedness result in secretion from sweat glands. These changes i.e. variations of skin resistance are measured through this electro-mechanical device. One or two electrodes are to be fastened either on the palm or on the foot finding out the sweat glands. The other electrode may be fastened either on the wrist or near the ankle. This instrument measures the reactivity of the skin of the examinee and thereby analyzing the sweat and skin resistance. deceptiveness is gauged.

In India, of late Polygraph test has become much popular and even the court's approval in this regard is being obtained. As an evidence, the court is yet to totally accept these scientific reports. Let us analyse the position in Indian laws. Sec. 25 of the Indian Evidence Act: "No confession made to a police officer shall be proved as against a person accused of any offence." Sec 26 of the I.E. Act, "Confession by accused while in custody of police not to be proved against him, unless it be made in the immediate presence of a Magistrate." Sec. 162 CrPC and Sec. 313 CrPC also reflect aspersion on the police investigators. Sec. 162 lays down that the statements recorded by the police in the course of an investigation shall not be used for any other purpose of contradiction. The expert findings in the Polygraph test are based on certain physiological discharges made by the examinee while replies to certain crucial and non-crucial questions.

Eventually as these examinations are done by the experts and not by the police officers, the limitations of both Sec 25 of the Indian Evidence Act and Sec.162 CrPC will not be attracted. But the examinee remains covered under Art 20(3) of the Constitution of India wherein "no person accused of any offence shall be compelled to be a witness against himself", is in vogue. The provision u/s 313 CrPC is not to incriminate the accused but to enable him to explain any circumstances appearing in the evidence against him. Lie detector test is found to break the interrrogee's deception and in the process with truth generation.

In some cases the mere presence of the suspect before a lie detector leads to voluntary confession without even an actual test. This test definitely proves to be a vital aid to interrogation. In some cases the Court has approved Polygraph test of the suspects and suspects consent are obtained.

PSYCHOLOGICAL STRESS EVALUATOR (PSE)

In this instrument the voice of the subject is taped in response to question put by the interrogators and immediately connected computer starts analyzing modulation of the voice. Experts give their findings evaluating the mode and scale of voice modulation.

When a man speaks, his voice transmits two types of modulations :

- Audible.
- Inaudible.

This inaudible modulation is not received by human ear. The PSE can decipher inaudible modulations as well. Thus inaudible modulations reflect internal stress, which are detected and measured by PSE. The subject would be asked to respond a series of questions, both truthful and deceptive, the deceptive can be detected. The PSE has got added advantage of examining taped telephone conversations too. This instrument is simple to operate as there is no appliance attached to it.

MARK 2 VOICE ANALYSER

Like PSE this instrument also records sub-modulation. It is also capable of processing taped telephone conversation and spoken words. This instrument can detect the stress oriented and deceptive kind of voice. It is very speedy and simple to handle. The quickness and simplicity are added advantage as compared to Polygraph.

TWO WAY MIRROR

A plain mirror on one side which permits a person on the other side to see through. A specially built mirror through which only the observant can clandestinely watch the movements and activities of the subject without his knowledge. Body language, activities, movements, soliloquy, reactions and actions of the subject can be monitored without the knowledge of the subject and the "concealed wisdom" of the subject. When a person is alone, he feels to act. This instrument is of much use during the breaks and in the rest periods.

BUGGING DEVICES AND MCR

Since taking direct notes during the process of interrogation is inadmissible, the help of modern science and technology has come to interrogator's rescue. Technically recording of conversations could be done both overtly and covertly. According to Harry Sodermann,"The detective who secures oral statements from a witness, suspect or defendant is often placed in a poor position in Court by having no record of such statements. In recent years a compact, efficient and economical device has been developed which assists the investigator in Court by making it possible for him to present a recorded transcription of his subject's remark." Therefore, the direct recording of the conversations can be operationalised. In this case, however, the interrogee would be conscious and he may keep himself reserved at crucial juncture. Once the subject is "broken," free flow of information continues. Now, with the development of science, technical recording is much easy and many small sophisticated devices including the MCR (Micro Cassette Recorder) are available. Not only from the point of handling but also these gadgets could also be concealed owing to their sizes. Ordinary tape recorder can also be used. In covert operation i.e. using of a mike concealed under any cover is the procedure. Wireless technology is used and the recordings could be carried on in an adjacent room which is technically termed as "safe house." Both recording and simultaneously hearing could be done by one interrogator placed in this room. Alternative power back-up is a must. Bugging can be done with or without laying any wire connection. As a precautionary measure, these gadgets should be tested prior to the arrival of interrogee. Changing of cassettes at the right juncture is a must. The microphone used is usually a very small and sensitive which can be concealed easily.

Indian laws are confusing over the fate of these recorded conversations. Tape-recorded conversation has been held to be admissible as a piece of documentary evidence [Pratap Singh v. State of Punjab AIR 1964 SC 72]. In Yusuf Ali v. State of Maharashtra (1968 CrLJ 103 SC) while admitting such a tape recorded conversation the Supreme Court observed, "The fact that tape recording was done without his (subject) knowledge is not of itself an objection to its admissibility in evidence." In saying so the Court does not lend its approval to the police practice of tapping telephone wires and setting up hidden microphones for the purpose of tape recording.

Where more than one suspects are lodged, putting up of bugging devices in that particular room and covertly recording their free conversation often provides clues and if necessary, could be played before the deceptive suspect to dislodge his deception.

The recordings on disc, tape or wire can be extremely useful in some cases, especially where the accused comes out with the allegations that his statement was obtained by threat or torture. In the case of hostile witness the recorded statement could be utilized to contradict him in the Court within the meaning of Sec 162 CrPC with the permission of the Court.

Most useful device found to be the Micro Cassette Recorder (MCR). In fact, each interrogator should be provided with this instrument along with cassettes back up. This small device could easily be concealed in one's pocket and only care is needed to change the cassette after 30 or 45 minutes without the knowledge of the person. Normally, the interrogator comes out of the interrogation room and does the necessary changing of cassette.

SENSITIVE CAMERAS AND CCTV

Sensitive cameras and Closed Circuit Television (CCTV) are gifts of modern technological developments. Both these two devices are used for overt and covert coverage of interrogation. These two instruments facilitate and monitor the total activities and behaviour of the interrogee both during the process as well as when he remains in the custody. In the open market, there are many handy and sophisticated cameras available which could easily be concealed in the concerned or targeted room. The concealment is done so carefully that the interrogee remains deprived of the coverage. Photographs obtained through this means are studied and examined. If needed, the interrogee is confronted with these clandestinely taken photographs. This process provides strong evidence and the interrogee is likely to be put off gear and his deceptiveness and other projected mannerism are exposed. The photographs obtained could also be produced, if permitted by the Court, as recorded evidence. The interrogators should be trained to carry out this operation and also to examine the recorded findings. After setting these cameras both the clandestineness and the proper functioning of each of them should be checked prior to initiation of actual operation. Number of cameras needed would be depending on the size of the room and the angles of coverage.

CCTV, now-a-days, has become much popular in security parlance. The mechanism and know-how further extends the use of this gadget. In interrogation too this electronic mechanism proves its worth. Both the verbal and non-verbal communications of the subject could also be clandestinely monitored from the adjacent room by an interrogator.

CCTV has also proved to be of immense help in monitoring the activities, conversations, behaviourism and mutual discussion of the suspects (more than one housed in a particular room). CCTV recordings are a very sensitive and effective piece of evidence, denial of which is near impossible by the suspects. This recorded evidence, at times, is produced in the Court in support of evidential value. In modern Interrogation Room, at the preparation stage, both the clandestine cameras and the CCTVs are installed. These in-built arrangements both from secrecy and operational angle are better suited.

P-300 OR BRAIN MAPPING

P-300 test is also known as Brain Mapping Test or Brain Finger Printing. It is a computer based technology to measure the brainwave responses of the subject to crime related words or pictures that can link the subject with the crime. In this test the accused first is interrogated to ascertain whether he has been concealing any fact or not. In case of deceptive subject, a sensor is attached to subject's head and he is seated before a computer monitor. He is then shown certain images or made to hear certain sounds. These sensors monitor electrical activity in the brain and register P-300 waves, which are generated only if the subject has some connection with the stimulus i.e. the picture or sound already shown. This technique is based upon the premise that brain retains all important information and whenever reference is made to a particular event by words or pictures, the brain recalls the event. A particular event is referred to the brain response. This event related response which is technically called Event Related Potential (ERP) is measured by the Electroencephalograph (EEG). ERP is specific to a particular event for a particular person, hence known as Brain Finger Printing.

Words or pictures related to a crime, namely photograph of murder weapon, model of car used in the crime, blood-stained clothes of the victim, etc. are flashed on a video monitor under computer control along with other irrelevant words or pictures. When these details obtained from the crime involved, which are within the knowledge of the perpetrator, a specific electrical brainwave response called MERMER (Memory and Encoding Related Multifaceted Electroencephalographic Response) is emitted by the brain of the perpetrator (i.e. the subject), which is measured in terms of P-300, meaning 300 milliseconds emission level. These MERMERs are measured non-invasively through a headband equipped with sensors. The brain of an innocent suspect will not emit MERMERs under similar circumstances. A computer analyses the brain response to detect these MERMERS and thus determines scientifically whether or not the specific crime relevant information is stored in the brain.

In 1995 Dr. Lawrence A. Farwell, Director of Brain Wave Science, IOWA developed this method which he termed MERMER. In this test, the brain recognizes noteworthy information connected with the crime. These are known as "target stimuli". P-300 matches the test projections with those of the already stored or recorded information in the brain. The experts can differenciate the wavelength or these impressions. Normally, a person having no connection or innocent individuals would not "store" such inputs in their brain.

The horizontal scales represent time in milliseconds (ms). The vertical scales represent wave aptitude measured in micro volts (mv) of electrical potential. The positive charge results from positive icons being discharged from the cells of cerebral cortex as they deactivate following their initial response to the stimulus. A single P-300 event can be reliably detected. So the results of many stimulus brainwave recordings are averaged to filter out noise and expose the signal.

Three types of stimuli are presented namely "targets", "irrelevant" and "probes". The targets are made relevant covering the crime context. Each stimuli appears for a fraction of a second. The subject is given a list of the target stimuli and instructed to press a particular button in response to targets and another button in response to all other stimuli. Since the targets are notable for the subject, they elicit a MERMER. Most of the non-target stimuli are irrelevant, having no relation to the situation under investigation. Within these irrelevant a few relevants, which are connected with the case, are mixed deliberately. The knowledge within the brain of the subject elicits effective MERMER. When the information tested is crime relevant, known to the perpetrator and the investigator, then information present implies guilt and information not within the ambit implies innocence.

Whatever might be limitations, P-300 test has got wide acceptance in the USA where the FBI is extensivly using this method of testification. In India too this test is gaining popularity. The Bombay High Court in a landmark verdict in the case of Ramchandra Reddy v. State of Maharashtra (2004 AIR MR CR 1704) upheld the legality of P-300 test. The Special Court dealing with cases under MCOCA, allowed the Special Investigation Team probing Telgi Fake Stamp Paper Case to conduct the P-300 test on Abdul Karim Telgi, the prime accused, in December, 2003 at the Karnataka Forensic Science Laboratory, Bangalore. The defence lawyers, in this case contested against this order of court on the ground of violation of the spirit of Art 20(3) of the Constitution of India.

DNA PROFILING

Deoxyribonucleic Acid (DNA) profiling or DNA Fingerprinting, is a positive gift to the forensic scientists in carrying out and determining the crime contour, both from positive and negativating endeavour. It has been acknowledged as a most pivotal tool for personal identification by examining and evaluating biological samples like body fluids, stains, tissues, teeth, bones, semen and such other samples collected from the scene of crime, arrested criminals, witnesses and the victims. DNA is found in all human cells except red blood cells, being confined to the nucleus and a few smaller cellular inclusions called mitochondria. When a DNA profile is carried out on blood it is the white blood cells which are used, not the red blood cells. In blood grouping, the red blood cells are tested.

Sample collection and preservation of the samples are most careful areas. Any error in this respect, is bound to influence the result, whether inadvertently or deliberately. Context of substitutions and covert intentions are the areas of significant concern because the forensic scientists shall concentrate upon the "samples" received. In cases where paternity or maternity disputes are involved, the blood sample collector should personally certify and identify the correctness of the individuals from whom the blood samples are being collected. Sample from a crime scene which would be forwarded for DNA profile, has to be handled with great care to avoid contamination. These include blood, saliva, semen, mucus, skin, hair or even a cigarette butt. The perpetrators may go in for artificial ingredients in the scene of crime, thus proper alertness needs to be maintained. Samples may be collected as early as possible and should not consume much time in sending process too. In rape cases, vaginal swabs collection require reasonable care and this should be collected by the authorized medical practitioners.

Two major areas in which DNA analysis is involved in court proceedings are parentage dispute and criminal cases. For man a parental dispute is a cause of stress, social position, prestige, reputation, family problem, blackmailing and financial hardship. For the mother, however, a wide range including chastity, stress, betrayal, financial difficulties, bickerings in the family, dishonesty and use of force are incorporated and they have to pass through both mental stigma and physical sufferings. Identity and rearing up of the baby are also concerned areas. In criminal cases, once the report is obtained from the scientists of their findings from a DNA sample, the very crucial area starts i.e. the interpretations, correct understanding and corroboration from the examinee. In recent times, the Courts are much serious over the DNA profiling but they cannot totally rely on the profiling report. They also seek for corroborative evidences in this regard. An expert can give an accurate statistic of probability while the Court is the final authority to declare innocency or guilt. In the case of DNA experts, their academic qualifications, the recognition obtained and the expertise are the provisos. The Court honours the addition contributed in the case.

7 Body Language

In the process of interrogation "body language" does occupy a marked place in breaking silence or deceptiveness of the subject if proper attention is paid to observe and monitor the prognosis made of the emanated symptoms. Body language is where the human body, its gesture posture, normal and abnormal physical behaviour and movements and few other significant or unwarranted messages communicate and speak of or emit some tangible expressions. The moot question remains how best the interrogators could identify and then adequately interpret these body emissions. Wrong interpretation, improper analysis and omissions may create problem, confusion, stumbling blocks and hindrances in the process. The performers i.e. the subjects, emit several emotions namely anger, love, hatred, sadness, bewilderment, happiness, excitement, repentance, affection, abhorrence and lust. Intimidation, social status, position boredom, confusion, fear, punishment apprehension are few other courses found stressing the subject and also responsible for orienting a confused state of mind. Adoption of defensive gesture and to keep himself away from the offence and the charges, therefore, are smartly carried out by the subject from the very outset of the interrogation. Chalking out a plausible and well thought cover story becomes a part of this gesture too. Interrogation is known as the battle of wits and winner is determined on the score of outwitting the other.

Body language are many namely genetic, learned, cultural signals, expressions, gestures which are unspoken language of the body. Such as "V" sign, a gesture projected through fingers, signifies "all correct" or "victory" signals. Similarly, with the help of fingers one can express "OK" or even "denial". Thumbs are other body elements which may also be used in translating language like "to stop", "to deny", "to cover up face", "to project anger" and also to "reflect revenge attitude". These reflections and their frequencies including repeatations are indicators of serious hues, etc. communicate non-verbal communications. Body language is something, if not total, obviously associated with the defence mechanism and deceptive attitude adopted by the subject. Open palm gesture is viewed as expression of truth, allegiance, submission and mostly honest. Unconscious gesture of open palm signifies expression of truth. Hiding of one's palm in the rear side is indicator of deceptiveness. Transformation of the palm as a fist, signifies control or positiveness. Anger is also reflected through fist gesture. Perspiring palm indicates nervousness. A controversial gesture is the hand shaking. There are many types of hand shaking and each denotes separate meaning. Whether the interrogators would response to this very gesture if extended by the subject, there are divergent opinions. One lobby is of the view that to demoralize and denote "inferior", the interrogator should refrain from this act. It shall produce "impact" over the psyche of the subject. He would be "cut to size". The tendency of the subject remains to dominate the scene which may be adversely affected. The other group opined that initiation process may be "strong" if started with hand shaking which means friendliness establishment. Whatever might be, hand shaking is very common mannerism. These gestures also require proper evaluation to estimate and apprise the subject.

Thus while we carry on interrogation, proper attention should also be paid to visualize his body actions and reactions and the total response of the body while reflecting answers or even keeping mum. During silence body also murmurs. CCTV coverage is thus considered as a very fruitful measure where, if necessary, the subject may be confronted with his own "body language". It is an effective technique to erase his deceptiveness or long silence.

The interrogators must be trained to detect, understand, signifies, estimate and confront.

VERBAL AND NON-VERBAL COMMUNICATIONS

Interrogation is a process of communication between the interrogator and the interrogee. Communication means and includes asking, receiving, consuming, confronting, evaluating pronouncement, admission, denial of, etc. in the form of pronouncement by way of verbal, non-verbal, symbolic, gesture, posture, body language and written forms. Dr. J. Rasicot opined that during face to face interrogation 10% is transmitted through words, 30% through voice inflection and 60% through non-verbal communications. The interrogators mainly lay more stress on question-answer part i.e. the revelations made, which may be treated as direct communication. We must concentrate on the body language i.e. the behaviour of which interrogees have less control or no control. These may be termed as vocabulary of the body or body language. There are wide range of physical reactions which are instinctive and beyond conscious control, i.e. spontaneous body reactions. Sigmund Freud, the famous psychologist, said, "He that has eyes to see and ears to hear may convince himself that no mortal can keep a secret. If his lips are silent, he chatters with his fingertips, betrayal oozes out of him from every pore". Interrogation is a face to face encounter and a battle of wits. It is a psychological game. Purpose is to elicit truth. Truthful people usually extend their body open, upright, settled, shoulders squared. Deceptive type persons are mostly closed, defensive, even they crossed their legs and arms. Tension affects the voice pitch and cracking. There is a distinct difference between "anger" and "covert anger". To understand the "guilt" part or deception both verbal and non-verbal communications could be of immense help. Chinese method of interrogation suggested that it is a known psychological fact that a person under extreme tension ordinarily have a dry mouth. Verbal behaviour is more controlled than non-verbal. We think before we talk.

By verbal we mean oral expressions whereas non-verbal behaviours are movement, posture, response and mode of the body i.e. the overt projection of the physical organs of which the subject has no control. These actions are controlled from central nervous system. Observations and interpretation of these behaviours are obviously difficult. Many times, no single behaviour by itself proves anything. Decisions need to be taken by combining both verbal and non-verbal modes of actions. To buy out truth not the body of the subject is the goal. To study brain's language may not be so easy process and hence requires specialized knowledge and experience. Deceptive subjects tend to deny their crime specifically, while the truthful one shall deny the crime in general. Deceptive person avoids realistic and harsh language. Truthful person normally answer specific questions with direct and spontaneous answer. Deceptive subjects consume times, take pause, sideline the question asked, they cultivate the culture of "delay tactics". They often request for repeating the question primarily to gauge intention of putting the question. They tend to distract the attention of the interrogators by swearing in the name of God, children, etc. They are overtly polite, can control their anger and are observant upon the behaviour pattern of the interrogators. The truthful subject is quick to anger and denial factors. At times, the deceptive interrogee starts with anger but graduation of interrogation progresses made him quiet. Increasing pulse rate is an indication of deception, while the subject tend to conceal truth, his breathing ratio also increases. Verbal behaviour encompasses the words that are actually spoken. The choice of words, language, tone of the voice and the speed of delivery are other cognizable factors.

Human Nervous System may be divided into :

a) Conscious and b) Unconscious (automatic) parts. Unconscious portion is further divided into - i) Sympathetic i.e. self preservation and ii) Parasympathetic i.e. house keeping of the body.

Some of the notable verbal communication modes are :

- Shaky voice.
- Voice cracking.
- Shuttering.

- Tooth grinding.
- Deep sighing.
- Repeats question.
- Shaking.
- Nervousness.
- Trembling.

Thus voice modulation, tone, volume, speed, pause, controlling, etc. need to be minutely observed.

Non-Verbal Communications :

The major forms of non-verbal communications are :

i) KENESICS - body movements which convey information in the absence of speech.

ii) OCULESIS - eye movement. Language communicated through eyes.

iii) FACIAL EXPRESSION - face reading.

iv) PROXIMITY - Distance in respect of time, space and relationship.

v) HAPTICS - Science of studying data obtained by means of touch.

Kenesics

Body movement of any hue, is an indicator of stress, fear and emits psychological as well as physiological reactions. Posture, gesture, body leaning, ambulation and such other signals, if interpreted correctly, answer many concealed questions. Knowledge about human physiology and behaviour is a must to address correctly these contours. In fact, over these physical movements and actions, the interrogee has got no control. Perspiration is a great indicator of stress and anxiety. Interrogators should look not only at the exposed portion of the body of the subject but specially forehead, palms of hands, under-arm etc. Excessive perspiration is definitely an indicator of deception.

Rubbing and wringing of hands, indicate nervous frustration. Pulling of nose, earlobes, hair, clothing, etc. emit signal of nervousness too. Scratching, stroking, picking and pinching are unconscious actions to relative tension and thus not allowed during the interrogation process. Crying, both real and contrived, denotes both tension reliever and adopting delay tactics. Chewing the lip, nails, gum, etc. are symptoms of nervousness. Sighs and yawns, are stress reliever and also indicate tiredness of the body. Clearing of throat and coughing indicate adaptation of delay tactics. Dry lip means deception and also of anxiety. The interrogee often adjusts his clothings to cover up his nervousness. Internal conflict of the subject may be gauged from shifting of the torso. Frontal alignment i.e. facing towards the interrogator is indicative of truthfulness. More relaxed and casual mood of the subject indicate truthfulness. Upright and straight sitting of the interrogee predict his truthful nature.

Some of the behaviour patterns are detailed below :

Behaviour Pattern	*Indicative of*
• Unnaturally rigid	Deception
• Lack frontal alignment	do
• Defeated posture	do
• Grooming hair repeatedly	do
• Tend to retreat beyond physical barriers	do
• Erratic changes in positive posture	do
• Upright sitting and comfortable positioning	Truthful
• More relaxed and casual	do
• Covering the mouth	Concealment
• Clearing the throat	Delay tactics
• Chewing lip, nails	Nervousness
• Wiping Sweat	Hideness.
• Rubbing or touching part of the body	Deception
• Trembling	Nervousness
• Playing with moustache	Nervousness
• Shaking	Tension

• Fainting	Tension
• Vomiting	do
• Sigh and yawns	Stress
• Crying	Tension reliever.
• Smoking	do

Few symbolic gestures are :

• Agreement	- Nodding the head
• Denial	- Head shaking
• Sincerity	- Open arms, palms up
• Disbelief	- Hands near chest
• Accusation	- By pointing finger
• Threats	- By showing fist
• Helplessness	- Hands Posture
• Disgust	- Turn the head away
• Avenge (by murder)	- Pointing finger (firing pose)

Oculesis

There is an old saying, "The eye is the window of the soul." 90% facial information generates through eyes. Normal eye contact is maintained between the interrogators and the subject approximately in the range of 30 - 60% during interrogation. Therefore blindfolding the subject during the interrogation is never recommended. Interrogators are having greater freedom in this respect. However, too long a gaze by an interrogator may be counter-productive if the subject accepts it as a challenge or threat. Truthful subjects look direct, open and for long duration while the deceptive interrogees avoid direct eye contact, often they close their eyes, give stale look and avoid eye-confrontation. The size of the pupil differs too. Excessive blinking of eyes are indicator of deception.

Facial expressions

Face is the index of mind. Even we observe a person first by looking at his face. During interrogation we primarily concentrate more on the face of the subject to understand the unexpressed versions. Facial expressions and changes help us in anticipating emotion, feeling, relationship, concern, stress, fear-psychosis, etc. of the subject. Sudden change of colour on the face is indicator of guilt. Unexpected and sudden questions change the colour of the face of the subject. In fact, these spontaneous reactions do generate automatically, having no control whatsoever. Sign of fear on the face is more indicative of guilt while cold stare is more indicative of innocence. Sad expressions and darkness (paleness) are pointer of deception.

Proximity

According to Dr. Edward T. Hall, Prof. of Anthropology, North Western University, distance relationships among people of varying degree of intimacy have a direct effect on a person's manner of relating. Interrogations are done in a controlled situation. Sitting arrangements are made as per requirement. However, the subject is never provided armed chair in order to deprive him from taking any rest. The distance zone between the interrogee and the interrogators is a subject of adjustment and need. Dr. Edward T. Hall conducted a research on proxemics. He suggested general distance between 3-4 feet.

He has divided the zones in four categories :

Intimate zone - within 1.5 feet. - still within touching distance

Personal zone - 1.5 feet to 4 feet.

Social zone - 4 feet to 12 feet and

Public zone - beyond 12 feet to 25 feet or beyond. It is public speaking distance.

Key concept of proximity is gaining psychological advantage. Violent criminals are uncomfortable at closer range. Interrogation is inter-personnel relations. Closeness thus play a pivot role in establishing rapport and understanding behaviourism of the interrogee. Deceptive suspects will unconsciously retreat from a threatening situation. He moves even his chair away from the interrogator. He prefers to sit near the door or window. Sometimes, the interrogee attempts to leave the room in any pretext, which may be minimized by positioning chairs and by denial. Deceptive subjects tend to keep themselves away from Bully or Human Vulture types of interrogators. Personal zone is just outside touching distance but close enough for personal discussion to take place. Social zone shall provide informal discussion scope. Normal distance be four feet and gradually move to intimate zone. Advancement of the interrogator to the proximity of the subject may produce fear and anxiety in the latter's mind. Deceptive subject's tend to maintain safe distance from the interrogators.

Haptics

This technique is adopted by hard criminals and deceptive type subjects. They try to be close to the interrogators and even touch their person. Inappropriate touch may inflict injuries to the interrogators. Repeated adoption of this technique is indicative of delaying the process and distracting concentration of the interrogators.

Respiratory pattern

It is considered as normal between 18 to 22 cycles per minutes. In case of deceptive subject the speed changes dramatically owing to fear of detection.

None of these modes can be taken guaranteed. These requires further elaboration and confirmation through oral revelations. Single observation is difficult to be relied upon. The team should come to a conclusion after threadbear analysis. However, both verbal and non-verbal communications, if observed and analyzed in the correct perspective, do generate unexpected result. The use of CCTV or clandestine cameras provide good dividend in monitoring these movements and activities. The recordings done by these clandestine gadgets, later may also be used in confronting and breaking the subject.

8 Documentation

The final stage of interrogation process is the preparation of the interrogation report (IR), which is also termed as documentation. It may be done in two ways, one by the interrogator and secondly, transcribing electronically generated and recorded versions and thereby processing the report. In both these two methods, human brains are necessarily involved in preparation of the final IR which is the projection, manifestation and modelling of the entire interrogation deal into few pages, thereby rendering it a complete, clear and readable document. The interrogee reveals and forward many topics, along with the cogent inputs. It is thus the responsibility of the interrogator to make differences between the necessary or relevant points and weed out the unnecessary or irrelevant parts.

It is the IR, which is tabled before the authorities, not the subject of interrogation. The evaluators adjudicate it on the merit or demerit of the concerned report only. The IR is written for the consumption of others, not of the interrogators. The prognosis of the entire case lies on the preparation of the report and eliciting of the actionable inputs like names, locations and other details of the co-accused, group members, recoveries including arms, ammunition, explosives, money, booties, lethal weapons, subversive literature, etc. Thus a comprehensive IR is regarded as a solid base by the investigator. Though the outcome of this process may be decided by others, but the role played by interrogators can never be tarnished or dis-regarded in any way on the ground of using their talents and tacts, reasoning, measuring sticks and efficiencies, to clear out falsehood, untruth, contradictions, confusions, unclear views, blocks and the fallouts. In the investigation process, the IR, thus, is reckoned as a solid base.

Recording (audio/video) of the process of complete interrogation is essential as any kind of writing or taking notes in front of the subject is not permitted. In fact, writing in front of the subject needs to be avoided owing to drawing attention of the interrogee who feels that the revelations made by him may go against him. Thus where there exists no scientific recording system, taking mental note and then jotting the revelations are suggested. Another simple method, where audio/video recording systems are not there, may be adopted where one member of the interrogation team may be positioned at the rear side of the interrogee who may take brief notes without drawing immediate attention of the subject. This interrogator is debarred from putting any question. He shall remain silent all along the process.

However, in case of confessional statement made voluntarily by the interrogee, the confession needs to be recorded. This type of confession is finally recorded before a judicial authority. Thus proper motivation, training are essential to avoid any kind of contradiction. No threat or coercion be there. This report must be systematic, logical and chronological in order. Actionable inputs may separately be jotted down as these would require immediate action. Proper attention be paid to extract maximum details. In the case of a person, his descriptive role and in case of a place exact location need to be extracted for operational angle. Where there is no house number, the location needs to be fixed by obtaining any significant landmarking. A sketch map better be enclosed.

The inputs provided by the interrogee must be verified through independent channel. In case of an information pertaining to jurisdiction not covered by that particular unit, reference may be made to the jurisdictional authorities for early verification of the information and also soliciting necessary details. In this case a point may be remembered that no direct enquiry be caused and the course of secret enquiry may be well guarded so that the follow up actions can be effectivated.

The Interrogation Reports in normal cases are official document but in case of CI suspects, counter-militancy or alike sensational cases, these are graded as "Secret". It is also mandatory to protect the revelations made during the process of interrogation. Exposure may jeopardize the prospect of the case. The IR must be written as per prescribed format and part-wise. It is a permanent record. Names of the persons and places should be written in capital words. In the comments portion, the interrogators can give their comments/observation otherwise it is a subjective report. IR is the composition of the factual revelations made by the subject and as far as possible in verbatim. Nowadays computer is used for recording IR and even, in many cases voice is also recorded for future reference or examination. It may be kept in such a way that it can be retrieved easily. Indexing may help quick record checkings.

There are three normal procedures viz. note taking, electronically recording and obtaining written confession (interrogee's own handwritten). There are other recognized tests like Narco-analysis test, Polygraph test, DNA profiling, P-300 test, etc. All these are undertaken in order to unearth the truth and to eliminate deceptiveness. While preparing IR, mention of any of these tests, if undertaken, be reflected., and all the test reports should be enclosed along with the IR. Similarly, the photographs, specimen handwritings (in all languages known by the subject), footprints, fingerprints, blood sample, voice recording, etc. should also be part of the complete IR.

A very significant point is writing DR (Descriptive Role) of the subject. All the necessary points need to be covered and recorded correctly including two prominent identification marks of the subject. The height should be accurately measured.

Taking mental note and preparation of the IR depend entirely on the memory of the interrogators. This process entails many hazards. Many significant points may not be incorporated for want of recalling factor. It is thus safer to note down salient and important points as soon as possible. Monitoring of verbal, symbolic and non-verbal communications and grilling the subjects over these body languages is a technique adopted in many cases. The emissions are not to be recorded, in details, but the results are to be mentioned with little reference to these signals. IR needs to be submitted in time and addressed to the concerned officer by name who has authorized interrogation. IR is normally a permanent document but its life may be determined and classified by the concerned officer too. Proper custody of this important record should be ensured.

Interrogation formats may differ from subject to subject but the main thrust should not undergo any change. There are separate formats for separate categories of the subject and it is not mandatory to cover all the points mentioned there. IR should not incorporate any negative version, which reflects the incapability of the interrogators. Needless to note that legibility is very important. It is better to write only on one side of the paper leaving sufficient margin, allowing space to the reviewer. References of all the enclosures be mentioned in the forwarding report. The IR should be signed by all the interrogators, though one may prepare it in consultation with the team members.

While preparing IR the following points should be kept in view :

1. It must be written in a clearly understood, simple and precise manner. Please keep in mind that report is an important document and the consumers are others who were not associated with the interrogation process.
2. It should be accurate, complete, verbatim and concentration be laid to highlight the important and significant points.
3. It is a part of evidence collection, thus it should be convincing, logical and based on facts.
4. Proper stress be given to each "words" uttered by the subject and these "words" be recorded and incorporated in the report, in verbatim.
5. Mind that quality of the report not quantity matters. Thus report should be prepared logically, consequentially,

systematically, categorically, para and sub-para-wise, so that a complete picture is emerged.

6. Adequate focus is required to ensure that there is no distortion or omission of facts, inaccuracy, error in understanding and interpretations, lost information and observation defects. Imagination has got no scope in the report. It is a record of the close facts. Do not quote any thing which the subject has not uttered. Accuracy is the sign of trustworthiness of the report. No scope of misinterpretation of the facts. Fictions have no place too. In fact the relevant portions only be incorporated. The IR should be crystal clear and be founded on truth. Unclear inputs, unfounded revelations and the needless elaboration of purposeless matters may be avoided.

7. The names, with code names of the individual, places, etc. should be clearly spelled and be recorded in capital words. In case of any unknown or new place/address, a sketch map, locational details be referred in order to easily reach/ spot the location.

8. Never rely on your memory alone. Consult other interrogators in case of any discrepancy. It is better to recheck from the subject in case of any confusion during writing the report.

9. Never be hesitant to write the revelations made by the subject against any erring police or other such officers, politicians or person of repute. The exact revelations be noted with necessary details referring the complicity and involvement.

10. Tape recorded versions be written first in verbatim and then it may be edited as per requirement. The tape-recorded versions, short-hand books, CCTV coverage, etc. are the documents, which are required to be preserved till the final culmination of the case. These recorded versions may also be produced in the court of law as evidences, if needed.

11. Subject often reveal certain "codes" used by them in their profession and business. Codes should be written in local or their (subject's) language, providing English rendering in

the bracket. The new names of the streets, lanes etc., be mentioned giving the old and the popular local names in brackets. Special attention to be paid in using abbreviations. Only the recognized one is used, not the improvised one.

12. IR of each subject be prepared separately. Forwarding memo or note of a group or several arrests in one case, may be one.
13. Use of vocabulary and long sentences including "hard words" be avoided. The words are to be communicative and better understood. Language has got a meaning.
14. Inordinate delay in submitting IR is not warranted. It should be done as early as possible. The more the delay, the more the loss of memory and sequences.
15. All the interrogators should sign the IR.
16. Information catered by the subject may be usually in piecemeal. It has to be jotted, collated and summed up in a paragraph.
17. Respectability, perceptibility and visibility factors of the interrogators, specially to translate into writing certain verbal, non-verbal and electronically extracted exposures are few marginally anticipated flaws. In fact these actions, omissions and behavioural reflections need to be confronted and after having filtered through the interrogee, the recording ought to be made to derive at a correct conclusion. Here comes the trustworthiness and acceptability of the report.
18. No casual approach while preparing the IR. Proper attention and focus are necessary.
19. Secrecy of the IR is another point of demand. The IR may be enriched with several actionable inputs and thus the report is required to be safeguarded from leakage.
20. Often the interrogee is told to prepare interrogation report of his own. It reflects his self-intellect and capability. He may have inadvertently missed few points.
21. These reports may or may not be acknowledged in the Court of Law but the subject may be in two minds if the

report is obtained without any pressure, threat or torture. The prime focus is on voluntary admission which may be reason based.

22. The IR may be written in the first person and the simple narration of the fact revealed by the interrogee. It should be written in the language of the subject and in his own words. Sometimes, question-answer form may also be used for better reflections.

23. IR should preferably be written neatly and clearly in one side of a sheet of paper, regardless of the volume. Enclosures like photographs, specimen handwriting, blood sample, foot and finger prints, voice recording etc. be clearly noted in the forwarding note. Each page of the IR should be numbered.

24. IR is a permanent record. Some time the record is security graded too. Thus these records be kept under custody and easy retrieval also be ensured.

25. No unnecessary space be left. The rules of grammer are not essential. Accuracy, proper revelation and addressing the very purpose of the interrogation are the basic ingredients.

26. The Police Station's jurisdiction of each place be clearly recorded in the report.

27. Accuracy be maintained while writing the DR of the subject. Special mention be made in case of any special feature, deformity or marks.

28. IR is the reflection of a teamwork not projecting of an individual skill. In case of any difference of opinion, the same may separately be reflected for office use only. This sort of reflection should not reach the Court.

29. Each recoveries made, should be vetted during interrogation and details need to be obtained. These may be incorporated in details, in the IR.

30. Electronically recorded statements may be properly checked and changes in the voice pitch, tone and audibility, if found, be minutely observed. The CCTV coverage

further adds the pictorial projections like anger, frustration, remorse. The recordings may be, on demand, forwarded to the court. And may be treated as crucial evidential value. The cassettes, used in the operation, are also be treated alike manner.

31. Special care be taken to make documentation of the IR of the victims. The secrecy in certain cases may strictly be maintained. Camera trial is not mandatory in sexual offences like rape (Sec. 376 IPC) and other such offences. Any one who publishes the name of the victim of a sexual offence, or publishes the court proceedings, without requisite permission, is liable to be punished with imprisonment of either description which may extent to 2 years and shall also be fined. (Sec. 228 A IPC).

Descriptive Role (DR)

Writing of descriptive role (DR) of the subject in the Interrogation Report is compulsory. It should be in details and close to accuracy. However, this process is devoid of any guessing or conjecture. If required, close observation or measurement be taken. In fact, the interrogation provides scope for close and correct visual observation as the subject remain within the reach of the interrogator. In interrogation room provisions for obtaining accurate height and weight should be there. The DR of the subject should be elaborately written. R-SHAH+2 i.e. Race, Sex, Height, Age, Hair plus two other significant visual physical marks in the body of the subject are normal requirement. While writing DR of any individual mentioned by the subject, proper care and caution need to be taken.

Let us now analyze different contours of the significant points, which are to be incorporated in the DR :

RACE : Indian, European, Chinese, etc. (It will be difficult to differentiate between the Indian, Bangladesh or Pakistan nationals. Interrogation will provide scope to ask his nationality).

SEX : Male, female and hermaphrodite.

AGE : Date of birth should be noted. In absence, approximate age be recorded. Place of birth is equally important.

HEIGHT : Exact measurement be taken.

BUILD : Normal, strong, medium, heavy, light or fatty.

HAIR : * Colour like black, brown, grey, white, partly white.

* Baldness,

* Size like short cut, long, thin, thick, curly, excessive long parted in the middle, etc.

HEAD : Normal, flat in rear side, abnormally large, turban, using any cap or hat.

FOREHEAD : Broad, medium, narrow, receding, vertical, prominent, etc.

EYES : Black, brown, blue, small, large, sunken, bulging, squint, one-eyed, blind, special mention be made about wearing of specs and any eye deformity. Specialities of the eyebrows, if any.

NOSE : Pointed, turned up, twisted, turned downward, and nostrils specialities.

LIPS: Thick, thin, protruding.

TEETH : Colour, composition, missing, protruding.

CHIN : Double, dimpled, square, large, long, normal, receding, pointed.

EARS : Large, medium, small, round, oval.

FACE : Oval, square, round, prominent, bonny, prominent jaw, sunken cheek.

NECK : Long, short, thin, thick.

MOUSTACHE : Clean shaven, thin, bushy, butterfly.

COMPLEXION : Fair, wheatish, black, brown.

CLOTHES/WEARING : Suit, trousers, and shirt, payjama-kurta, dhoti and kurta, hat, half-pant, T-shirt, lungi-banian, shoes/

Chappals. Colour of dress (Special attention be laid on maker's mark).

DISTINCTIVE MARKS : Scars, moles, marks, birth-marks, cut-marks, missing fingers, pockmarks, operation marks. Walking gait.

DEFORMITIES : Lameness, pot-bellied, missing finger, 6 fingered, hunchback, stooping, stammering, one-eyed.

Photograph

Each IR must incorporate 3 photographs of the subject, one front view and two from the two sides. It may be black and white or in colours. At the back of the photographs the name and case reference of the subject should be written. Never write anything on the photograph which may deface the same.

9 Memory — Loss and Retrieval

Loss of memory is a general complaint preferred by criminals during investigation. The purpose may be adoption of dodging technique as well as genuine owing to sudden shock, upsetting of mind and mental fever. Memory is one of the most sought after criterion in the interrogation process as the subject is required to recapitulate the entire episode. A lot of thinking process and recallings is also involved. Forgetfulness hinders the investigation process too. The relation between memory and forgetfulness may be compared with the light and darkness. Memory, in general, is the retaining of the acquired experiences in the mind and forgetfulness is when we fail to retrieve these treasured facts.

Memory refers to :

i) A mental function of retaining information about stimuli, events, images, ideas, actions, activities, etc. after the original stimuli are no longer present.

ii) The hypothesized "string system" in the mind or in the brain that holds the information, and

iii) The information so retained. Memory is a complex process in psychology and therefore we should understand the entire process and the blocking waves.

Acquisition is the primary phenomenon in the process of learning. S. Stevens defined acquisition as a progressive incremental change in the proficiency of performance by an organism. The direction, rate, and extent of change in the proficiency of performance are function of repetitive or continuous presentation of conditions under which the measurement of change in performance is met. In fact, this primary component rests and relies on length, difficulty, ambiguity, meaning, usefulness, emotional appeal, motivation, positioning of the input as well as factors like age, sex and physical condition of the retainer. Every experience leaves behind it certain resided disposition or traces which are retained and helps subsequent recall. The four factors involved are recall, recognize, retention and remembering. Recall may be immediate or delayed.

There are various modalities in memory. Iconic memory which is also known as visual memory or visual information storage or perceptual visual memory, is defined as a residual sensory memory that lasts for a short time after a brief usual stimulus. It is considered by many to be one of a class of phenomena within the sensory information store. It decays rapidly with time, duration is affected by display contrast, not playing proper attention when displayed and the information is not translated from image. Echoic memory is a residual sensory memory that lasts for a short time (perhaps 2-3 seconds) after a brief auditory stimulus. It is regarded as a recalled signal. That's why in a series of display, only last few items could be recalled. Short Term Memory (STM) provides a temporary resting place for information from sensory memory that we have attended to. It is a process between sensory storage and Long Term Memory (LTM). Chunking i.e. a process of grouping items, is adopted for easier remembrance as the information in STM is in acoustic form. Waugh and Norman performed a study when they interpreted their findings as showing how information in STM is continually being replaced due to retention capacity and new information coming in replacing the old ones. STM forms the first stage for LTM and that information transferred from one to the other by rehearsal. Memory of information that has been well processed and integrated into one's general knowledge store, is called Long Term Memory (LTM). It is like a giant store, which accumulate facts, feelings, images skills, etc. and are never filled. Chunks of information are stored, there is no known limit, everlasting and even for lifetime. LTM may be categorized as procedural memory, declarative memory, episodic memory and sematic memory. In both the STM and LTM "control process" play dominant part and the people, in general, rely on flexibility, voluntarily depending on material and their personal preferences. Rehearsal is another modulation to keep these intact and there are less possibilities of being "lost". There may be superficial processings and may occur invalid findings. In 1890 William James observed that we seem to possess more than one kind of memory, viz. ordinary, lasting and rapid. This rapid memory is likely to fade very quickly. There are few aspects like spaced learning, whole versus part learning, active versus passive learning, coded learning, etc. which do harbour their individual prospects too. Over-learning, review, memory training, feedback, flashback are few memory state depending process. "Black-outs" is often caused owing to internal physical disintegration like heavy consumption of liquors, etc.

LOSS OF MEMORY

Let us now discuss the reasons behind loss of memory/forgetfulness and how to improve one's memory. Forgetting is, broadly speaking, the loss of ability to recall, recognized or reproduced that which was previously registered. It refers to apparent loss of information, which are encoded and stored in long term memory. Different views give different justification for the phenomenon of forgetting. The levels of processing theories would blame lack of rehearsal or inadequate encoding. Traditional learning approach, as per Dallen Bach, would call it "weaking of associated bonds". Psychoanalytic theory treated forgetting as result of repressions. According to Gestalt : Theory forgetting is viewed as the result of disruption or interference with short term memory.

Factors/reasons

Natural decay of memory may occur due to various reasons. The psychologists and neuro-physists are on continuous research to annihilate these blocks or factors. The advancement of science and technology and the change in behavioural conceptions might help in combating these menaces. However, we may discuss few known reasons as under:

i) *Short Term Memory* has limited capacity. These are treated as "irrevocably gone".

ii) *Long Term Memory* is theoretically unlimited memorial system but there are many conditions for loss or damage in this system too.

iii) *Lack of Interference* : If one cannot grasp or follow the object then there may be erase in retention. Thus while recalling, the memory may not be retrieved either. One should properly understand the subject matter and should also conceptuate accurately and correctly. Otherwise, there may be total gap in registering or sorting.

iv) *Brain Damage* : Brain damage or memory disorder known as amnesia can happen in different ways ranging from organic damage, head injuries to problems arising due to ageing. It is also difficult to be sure whether the genesis of forgetting is in amnesia or normal forgetting. Severe blows or wounds to the head, can result in loss of memory. Any kind of accident causes post-traumatic amnesia. Retrograde amnesia is when owing to brain disease or injury, one is unable to trace. Even though they can retain these memories before the damage. Antergrograde amnesia means missing links. While the patient is suffering from Karsakoff's Syndrome, he is unable to recall the names of the staff working under him.

v) *Ageing* : Though ageing is considered a factor but it cannot be generalized as many aged people do not suffer from this syndrome at all. Harris and Sunderland, who conducted researches on this point, opined that younger people experience more memory failure than the older ones. Retired people have less active lives than younger and they have less to remember in the first place. In fact, the forgetfulness of the younger people, which is higher, go unnoticed of the aged people who have this problem, use memory aids strategies, habits, rest etc. People affected with Alziemer's disease have this problem. However, the decrease of certain physical responses and some effect of the age, do damage or affect memory too.

vi) *Motivated forgetting* : Freud considered forgetting due to repression. According to him, memories become buried in the unconscious state. Repression is the key, though a chain of associated ideas lead to traumatic memory. Certainly our emotions do seem to affect memory. Emotional experiences, pleasant or unpleasant, stand out in memory. It seems that we tend to spend more time in emotional event and thereby more attention is paid to memorize it.

vii) *Interference* : The idea that while a new input or information get registered, either it interferes with the earlier one or provocates to forget the existing memory resulting in keeping the older one at bay. These factors contribute to forgetting. Interferences also cause extra thoughts and may not allow existing memory to remain unless they are strong. New learning may internally interfere with the old learning, which is known as retroactive inhibition while in the case of proactive inhibition, learning occurs before the learning in question and interferes with the recalling.

viii) *Distortion* : It may also be viewed as a distortion of what was previously experienced. Traces of previous experiences are somehow altered in the course of their interactions with other traces. They were able to show that there were regular kinds of distortion that occurred during the retention internal.

ix) *Retrieval failure* : Not all information that is stored is retrievable. Endel Tuluing, who is a very active researcher in memory processes, has suggested that the means for retrieval of information are usually established when the information is stored. If appropriate retrieval cues are not established at storage stages, then retrieval becomes much difficult.

x) *Consolidation theory* : According to consolidation theory trace needs time. Certain conditions which occurr soon after an experience can eradicate the memory before it becomes permanent.

xi) *Physical shock :* When electro-convulsive shock occurs immediately after learning, forgetting chances are maximum. Any kinds of sudden physical shock affects the memory.

xii) *Emotional shock* is another psychological factor, which may cause temporal or permanent loss of memory. The gravity and amount of shock should be the core factor. The effect of this type of shock is tremendous and even can make an individual mentally paralyzed.

xiii) *Maturation :* The maturity of the person to grip the subject, things, feelings, topics and events are other factors. If the retention is not proper, then how the full recall be done. One should be fully matured to store the knowledge in right perspective so that it can be recalled, remembered or retrieved when needed.

xiv) *Fatique :* Fatique is another factor, which not only affect the physical aspect but also the mental phenomenon too. When an individual is otherwise tired he cannot pay proper heed or attention to any other subject or topic.

xv) *Medication :* Drugs, alcohol and narcotic substances are reasons for the loss of memory. That's why when any interrogee is subjected to Narco-analysis test (Truth Serum Test) he looses his normal defensive mood owing to the influence of the administering of certain specific drugs, namely Scopolamine, Penobarbital, Evipan, Moephine, Sodium Amytal, Chloroform, Seconal etc.

xvi) *Length of the task :* Lengthy things create boredom. One becomes unable to keep his constant attention over all the points. Thus when the process is too lengthy, there are probabilities of less remembrance. He can retrieve only the significant points, which have registered his attention. If a person is shown 50 items at a stretch, he can name only a few of them.

xvii) *Ambiguity :* If the contents of the matter are not easy to comprehend, or carry a dual message or conception, which in turn confuses the sender, then the ambiguity of the message acts as a hindrance in acquisition. The matter or the contents of the matter may be interpreted in the particular way in which the individual practices it. Ambiguity thus is another factor when the acquisition is highly corrupted. Acquisition is correlated with the number of responses for which the subject receives knowledge.

xviii) *Poor fixation* : Failure to remember a name either of individual or a place, is due to poor fixation at the first instance. The important and non-important factor or the interest produce effective score in storing these in memory. Theory of association may help in recalling these from the storing memory. Occupation, physical feature, family connections and age are four outstanding traits to remember.

IMPROVEMENT OR RETRIEVAL OF MEMORY

The following measures may be useful in retrieving lost memory :

1. Developing of memorable links between different bits of information i.e. one item automatically leading onto the next.

2. Organizing information in a structured way helps to provide cues for retrieval.

3. *Encoding and processing* : It has been established that elaborating materials should be restructured or thinking encoded about their implications, to facilitate easy remembrance.

4. *Decay theory of memory trace* : One of the earliest ideas of memory storage was that remembered item would leave a kind of psychological memory trace in the brain known as engram. Unless this engram is strengthened by rehearsal, it would gradually become weak and eventually fade owing to lack of use. Recalling or recognizing the items again would refresh engram. We cannot possibly know the existence of memory unless we try to use it. He even tries to produce a plausible reconstruction. In some cases of brain damage patients have produced evidence that memories may not decay permanently, even though the person may not remember. Socks, a neurologist, described that an 88 years old woman lived in the US since the age of 5 years after her mother's death, was unable to recall her early

childhood in Ireland, although she had often tried. After a mild Thrombosis in the temporal lobe, she suddenly began to hear Irish songs in her head. Neurological investigations emerged that these songs were retrieved memory of her mother singing to her in early childhood. As she recovered from the stroke the songs faded away. This case and many other such cases proved that there may not be complete decay but may be dormant instead.

5. *Overlearning :* Better it is learnt, the greater the chances of survival. Practice continues even after perfect learning is achieved. The more the revision, the effect of remembering would be better.

6. *Meaningfulness of the subject :* If the meaning of the subject is well understood, it can register and be retrieved easily. Unclear or not understood or vague subjects are not properly stored. Thus these cannot be retrieved at will.

7. *Use of organizers :* Systematic learning, sequential events and organized events be better retained. Thus students while learning do maintain a system for easy remembering. This clustering process is very useful in memorizing too. Context, cues and processing when done in similar settings, recalled easily. Few other bases like grouping, cues, method of location i.e. place etc., attention to meaning and secondary association are other cognizable factors. The deeper the thought, better the recall.

8. *Self recitation :* Through this system one can store and retain memory. Recapitulation and self expressions help in storing memory.

9. *Whole v Part :* When the matter is huge, it may be parted and then remembered. By way of adopting the whole is stored and can be recalled either in whole or in parts as per requirements.

10. *Feedback :* In this process one can test his own memory, recapitulation capacity and also learn the missing part and again store in the memory. Feedback thus help in recovering and refilling the lost memory.

11. *Concentration :* If proper concentration is paid, then systematically one can reach to the time when the storage was done and he can recall the memory back.

12. *Keen observation :* This quality in any individual not only helps in storing the memory sequentially but also protect any damage or loss owing to powerful observation power.

13. *Interest :* It is an instinct, which is also of fundamental need in memory game. Disinterest creates lackadaisical tendency. Interest is equally important in learning and remembering process. Loss or decay of memory can be prevented if proper interest is taken.

14. *Reviewing :* By reviewing, repeating, testing, discussing and rehearsing memory can be sharpened. In this process the missing link can be traced, the old one can be refreshed and thus memory can be strengthened.

15. *Using memonics :* It is another technique to prevent or block damage or loss of memory. It helps proper storing.

16. *Avoiding overindulgence in alcohol, narcotics :* Narcotics, drugs, alcohol etc. damage human nervous system and affect memory too. These should be avoided or consumtion should be limited. It is wise to avoid consumption of all these substances and enrich the memory. Negatively, certain drugs are used in the Narco-analysis test to cause effect in the human nervous system and extract the "concealed part" of the case which the subject is unwilling to part with.

INTERROGATION CASES

Apprehension by the police causes a serious mental shock to many arrestees. They become mentally upset and perturbed as soon as apprehended. They do often suffer from bewilderment and loose reasoning capabilities too. Loss of memory thus is an usual phenomenon. We have dealt, in details, about different pros and cons of retaining, recalling and blocking of memory. In the cases of interrogee too all these are equally applicable and they are also affected with all these phenomenon.

The following few additional methods may be useful to retrieve loss of memory of the interrogees:

a) *Association theory* : We have already discussed about the role of association theory in storing memory and also to recall them when needed. When any interrogee suffers from loss of memory and is unable to recall, recognize or remember, this association theory may bring his recalling capability back. During the process of interrogation, the interrogee often cannot remember the exact date or name or event due to his mental disorder. A good interrogator uses association theory to knock his memory door. As for example, if the subject is unable to remember his exact date of infiltration into India, he may be gradually asked the season i.e. winter, summer, rainy etc. or whether the pass through which he came (infiltration route) was snow clad, or there was water etc. or he may be asked about the dress he wore. This way first the month, then the proximate date etc. be ascertained. Sometime the remarkable days or black days like Ramzan, Christmas, Dussehra, Dec 6 (Babri Masjid Demolition Day), Diwali, etc. are referred as associated events.

b) A very significant point to note is that there are many facts or activities reckoned to be unimportant by the subject, may be of interest to the interrogators. During the process of interrogation, the interrogee, thus, cannot provide details as it has not been registered in proper direction in his memory.

c) *Scene of Crime Visit* : Visit to the scene of crime is another method by which the lost memory of any accused can be retrieved. Once he is again put in the situation, the situational condition promotes remembering or recalling the past events. By seeing dead body of the victim, sufferings of the victim, damage done by him, victim's or his families outcry, etc. his memory sensory is hammed, tensiled and he regains his recapitulation power.

Creation of simulated scene of crime is also applicable to retrieve his lost, damaged or derailed memory back.

10 Interrogation of the Naxalites

Naxalite problem at present is India's gravest threat to internal security. To quote Prime Minister Manmohan Singh, 'not a day passes without an incident of Leftist extremism taking place at some place or the other'. Elaborating the alarming network of Naxalites, Ajit Doval, a former Director of the Intelligence Bureau (IB) had stated that Naxal activity affects approximately 40 per cent of the country's landmass and at least 35 per cent of the total population.

The equitable distribution of land is the main demand of the Naxal outfits and this is the well pronounced policy of all successive governments as well. The report of the expert group (EG) on "Development Issues to deal with the Causes of Discontent, Unrest and Extremism" associated with the Naxalite movement, set up by the Planning Commission in 2006, has in its report, 'Development Challenges in Extremism affected Areas', put forth the new approach that Naxalism is a political movement with a strong base among the landless and poor peasantry and adivasis, which, "in its day-to-day manifestation" is seen by its support base as "basically a fight for social justice, equality, protection and local development."

The basic thrust of the different outfits is also to focus attention on the grievances of the people, inequalities suffered by large segments of the population, release of victims of exploitation from the tentacles of the landlords, etc. and to inculcate 'class' responsibilities among the economically and socially deprived sections. In pursuance of these objectives, the groups have not only mobilized the people but have also ensured that distributive justice is available in a rough and ready manner. The peoples' courts organized by these groups expropriate surplus land from the landlords to be distributed to the landless, dispense criminal justice, settle disputes and punish offenders. Thus, 'Jan Adalats' constitute a cornerstone of their efforts to win over the masses, particularly in the rural areas. Besides, they indulge in extortion from businessmen, contractors, traders, government officers, etc., and resort to murders and kidnappings to eliminate interference by agents of the established administration and defiant class enemies.

Various LWE groups have their presence in different parts of the country, notably the heartland states including Andhra Pradesh, Bihar, Jharkhand, Madhya Pradesh, Chhattisgarh, Maharashtra, West Bengal, etc. The CPML-PWG is well entrenched in almost all districts of AP, several districts of central and south Bihar, Jharkhand, southern districts of MP, Chhattisgarh and Orissa and a few eastern districts of Maharashtra and three districts of West Bengal. The most afflicted districts have gone to the newly created state of Chhattisgarh. It also has a presence in a few districts of Karnataka and Tamilnadu.

Thus, Naxalism continued and resurfaced in Nineteen-nineties and onwards with more vigour and better organizational capability in other parts of India and is still continuing in full bloom. In India, Naxalite movement covers about 80 million landless people and 30 million tribals. At present, Naxalites seem to have derailed from their main path of resistance movement. Their actions and spurt of activities have caused serious repulses. As a result, some counter measures or steps are necessary to wipeout/contain the LWE menaces.

INTERROGATION

Interrogations of the Left Wing Extremists (LWE) also called Naxalites are now-a-days rampant throughout the country as their activists are fanned out and no boundary can be made. Primarily it is the district police forces who are engaged in conducting preliminary interrogation soon after the apprehension. It may be taken into account that on the spot interrogation is much effective so far as the extremists are concerned, as most of them suffer from bewilderment and apprehension of elimination. Nevertheless interrogations remain one of the solid avenues to collect intelligence as normally penetration into the very fabrics of the formation is difficult. Another stumbling block is the open coverage in the media of the apprehension, and the entire network becomes sensitized and even go underground. Pressure is also mounted for the release through the Human Rights Organizations, and such fronts who try to air innocence of the arrestee and make lots of hue and cry. Side by side legal actions are also impounded as these activists are quite aware of procedural checks and bounds.

Left Wing Extremists are totally subverted individuals with high degree of motivation. They are subverted on ideological lines on MLM theologies. Once they are indoctrinated, it remains near impossible to dislodge their beliefs and conceptions. Their dedication and commitments towards the cause may be gauged from the fact of their leaving homes and leading miserable lives in the remote areas. They are used to immense sufferings. Extremist elements are fairly intelligent and in their leaderships there are many brilliant students who have left their studies and abandoned prospects for the cause. The training imparted to them is rigorous in nature. They are mostly trained in guerilla warfare and accustomed with the local conditions. Daringness and loyalty to the party are negative factors in the process of interrogation. They also prove to project personal position and normally do not respond to the interrogator's temptations. Many of the subjects in this category may outwit interrogators on account of their merit and brilliancy. As the organization professes restrictive security and functions in different layers. one individual member, thus, may not be privy to total information. Individual (arrestee) may only posses his limited knowledge and only the role played by him. This limitation is but natural in many cases. As the cadres are motivated on communist ideology they are normally prone to promote dialogue and tend to contradict which are opposed to their line of thinking. This talkativeness is otherwise a positive pointer to create urge in the mind of the subject. The more he shall talk, the more contradictions are likely to flare up. The intelligent interrogators, having perfect knowledge, in the process of longer discussion are likely to provoke the subject and willy nilly extract the desired inputs. The education level too may provide advantage to subjugate the subject by drawing a line between the reality and the theory. Not achieving the goal is another line of attack to break the resistance of the interrogee. Questions need to be carefully put and pressure mounted to obtain reply to significant points in order to confuse and corner the subject. It may be noted that the extremists are generally egoistic and blind in their thinking. Experienced interrogators always try to break the ego complex and the battle of wits start. Interrogation is a psychological war and besieged with many contours. Many comrades owing to their prolonged underground life and total alienation from the family as well as from the society as such, become psycophant and even mentally imbalanced. The stress, fear, conflicts in the party, confinements and unfulfillment of their objectives do act on them. Fear of elimination is a major factor at the early stage and intelligent interrogators may utilize this angle in order to break the subject and elicit desired inputs. The leadership crisis, inner bickering and personal contradictions apart from differences are few touchy points to outwit the subject. A sound knowledge of the present state of health of the organization is of paramount importance.

Nevertheless the interrogation of the LWE elements is a tough job mainly to those not familiarized with these elements. It is considered as a specialized task and updated knowledge on the subject is a must. The scenario in this field is changing rapidly. Modus operandi has also been changed. Adequate taking of cover and garnering of local support are matters of concern for the investigators. Language may often pose hindrances at the initial stage as members of this organization are drawn from several states. Another cautionary part is to provide adequate protection to the arrestee as his own party may try to eliminate him to seal disclosures.

The following points may be kept in view while interrogating LWE subjects:

1) Identification of the interrogee. Concealing of the real identity and using code names are common practices adhered by the extremists.
2) The cover story revealed by them at the initial stage may look convincing. This aspect requires to be verified.
3) The exact party affiliation should be confirmed together with the position held in the organization.
4) Reasons behind joining the outfit, mode of motivation and the name of the motivator may be ascertained.
5) Date and year of joining, initial tasking and activities carried out.
6) Locations visited.
7) Command structure of the party.
8) Details about frontal organizations and their locations.
9) Targets.
10) Funding channels, communication modes, linkages and nexus.
11) Overground activists.
12) Details about past actions.
13) National and international linkages.
14) Moles in the administration and police formations.
15) Details about the publications.
16) Arms holdings, strengths and training.
17) Recruitments.
18) Intelligence set-up.
19) Contacts with the press and media and also with the HR formations.
20) State of health of the organization.

The subjects under this category are indoctrinated people and as such they may not succumb to tortures. If treated humanly in the fashion of school master type of interrogation the fallout is likely to be positive. They require to be treated with rapid and continuous questions by the team so that no reprieve is availed. Sustained efforts and blow hot blow cold treatments are suggestive in order to create an urge in telling the truth. Emotional dependency may be carved out. Never try to castigate venom on the subject for commissioning of offences, even upon the police, always blame the system for the compulsion. Always give the subject a long rope, allow him to reveal what all he desires to and initially be a patient listener. Contradictions may be emanated from the utterings made. It may be clandestinely recorded. And if needed it may be played before him to dislodge. Always try to anticipate the reason behind the revelations. Unnerve him by putting abrupt surprise question of which the subject may not be mentally prepared. But care may be taken in putting such questions. The subject's endeavour may lie to ascertain the source of generating inputs on them. Exploiting the ego of the talented lots is common. Psychological approach may yield good result. Try to be friendly with him, never treat him as enemy. Raising of sources from among them are also the motto. Initiation and parting of interrogation are much significant.

11 Interrogation of the Terrorists

Terrorism, the term has its origin from the Latin word "terrere" meaning to frighten. The English words "terror" and "terrible" have the same origin. Throughout the history "terror" has been used as a technique to reinforce power and subjugate rule upon other. Therefore, terror and force cannot be separated. Another good definition of terrorism is threat or use of violence for political purposes by individual or groups, whether acting for or in opposition to established governmental authority, when such actions are intended to shock, stun, or intimidate a target group wider than the immediate victim. Terrorists can operate anywhere and at any time. Using terrorism is a low cost, low tech and high result route to a worldwide audience. Therefore, it is also called as low intensity conflicts or proxy war. It may be limited to a target or beyond that or even beyond state boundary. Many times the target location and the identity of the perpetrator remain under musk. Actions may be overt or covert. There must be mechanism to activate and translate the actions. Local assistances are other essential component. Often the terrorists operate from neighbouring countries or through allied nations. Both Bangladesh and Nepal are being used by the I.S.I. sponsored terrorist outfits as launching pads of the terrorist activities in India. Further the intelligence encirclements have been created by Pakistan against India which folded countries like Bangladesh, Nepal, Dubai and Myanmar. Political terrorism is mainly an endeavour to segregate a section of people, motivate them, psychologically and mentally pushed them towards a movement and finally an overture maligning the popular image of an established order. Terrorism may be state sponsored too. It is often sponsored and launched by one state against another by using violence and lethal force in the target area. Thus terrorism is an act of violence, done by a group or organization or even by an individual, in furtherance of their professed object or objects, with a view to terrorizing a government or establishment to engineer propaganda and/or to draw attention of international/national medias and to set their demands or causes.

Terrorism has donned the crime scene owing to the very fact that both from devastation and danger point of view, the challenges posed and the menaces have not only demoralized the security forces but shaken the very fabric of democracy. Complexed and vexed socio-economic-political compulsions, power conflicts, identity crisis, economic deprivations, corruption and mal-administration have further compounded the threat potentiality and in many cases, the very existence and functioning of the state systems have been under scanner. It has surcharged global security environment too. The entire security community is agoged and concerned about containment to these menaces. Problems are many. Terrorists of one country may be hero of another country. They are not confined to a particular area. Local support base of the transnational outfits is also there. They use both the conventional and non-conventional terror tactics. Transnational character further aggravate the scene as the real promoter remains behind the scene. Plannings are made in neighbouring countries and after commissioning of the act, the perpetrators exfilter to alien land for safe sanctuary. State sponsored terrorism is another agonizing factor. Whatever might be the scene or the theatre of the terrorist penetration, the state highly depends upon the police. Priority wise, in many states in India containment of terrorism is the most sought after responsibility entrusted to the police. In case of any ghastly terror act, the police is in the focus and consumes the blame. In crime investigation, specially in cases of terrorist acts, interrogations of the apprehended suspects are considered as a very potential measure in knitting and solving the case. Interrogations also help in thwarting many likely acts. Therefore, interrogation of the subjects under this head has got special significance and the role of the interrogators are prime attributing factor.

Terrorist acts are not confined to a particular crime. Majority of the crimes are heinous and fatal in nature. They often make calculated and planned attacks. Few are sporadic too. Targets may be selected by them but the ghastly acts often victimized the innocent and unconcerned people.

While interrogating a subject, the planning and preparation, total organisation details, sources of logistics, funding, local support bases, harbourers, communication systems, over ground supporters, etc. should be elaborately questioned.

Charasteristics of the terrorists

Attention may be focused upon the following characteristics:

- High degree of motivation.
- Totally dedicated towards the cause.
- Fairly high standard of intelligence.
- Rigorous training – both theoretical as well as arms – explosive handling.
- Trained in guerrilla warfare.
- Daring in nature.
- Use of most sophisticated gadgets and weaponry.
- Reasonably good educational background.
- Personal bravery.
- Tendency to sacrifice/fidayeen concept.
- Tendency to project himself as a role model.
- Garnering local supports.
- Knowledge of the area.
- Faster communication mode.

- Liaison with the Human rights and co-bodies.
- Religious indoctrination
- Working in cells.
- Trained in intelligence tradecraft.
- Secretiveness.
- Hatred for the police.
- Strong will power.
- Ambivalence towards authority.
- To generate propaganda.

Weaknesses of the terrorists

- High egoist. Thus can be provoked.
- Ideologically subverted. Once off geared, totally imbalanced.
- Education level – help to inflict reasoning.
- Prolonged underground life resulting to tiredness both physically and mentally.
- Bickering in the organization, if projected in right direction, produce convincing response.
- Feuds in the organization. If exposed in correct perspective, may bring the subject closer.
- Goal not achieved – may create frustation in the ranks and files.
- Leadership crisis or controvery. If lacunae can be exposed, the subject may be confused and may submit.
- Objectives may be unfounded, not realistic.
- Failing health of the subject. If well taken of, he may be won over.
- Psychologically imbalanced. Prolonged alienation, stress, fear, away from family may toll upon the psyche of the subject.

- Confinement and roped by the organization. Bringing back to the mainstream – proper rehabilitation programmes.
- Fear of elimination – both by the security force and by his own group members

During interrogation, stress may be laid to ascertain the real objective, purpose of targeting the particular person/place, planning and preparations in details, facilitators, communication modes used, hideouts arranged by, documents arranged by, funding made by, arms-ammunition-explosive provided by, advanced recce made by, names of the total team members, in case of death of any member his real identity, exfiltration route and other such vulnerable points. In case of retaliatory action the reason behind this action may be ascertained.

The reasons for joining as a member of the organization may be many. Interrogators should harp on evaluating the core cause in order to plug the same. Few common causes are :

- Unemployment
- Social alienation
- Poverty
- Corruption
- Economic exploitation
- Social exploitation
- Political cause
- Religious dogmatism
- Identity crisis
- Government's total neglect
- Racialism
- Communalism
- Caste struggle
- Class struggle
- Liberation struggle

- Power struggle
- Revenge
- Retaliation
- Police excsses
- Government decisions

Interrogation is not only confined to a particular case but it has wide spectrum. It is a very challenging job before the interrogators. Let us discuss the pertinent difficulties as well as the measures or techniques to be adopted to overcome the obstacles. The first hurdle is the knowledge about the organization, of which the subject is a member. Mushrooming growth of organizations and frequent changing of names are nevertheless a most challenging phenomenon. The police is mainly acquainted with and exposed to local organizations. Specially trained intelligence officers may be posted with the updated and detailed knowledge about these organizations. But prior to taking up interrogation, in case of an unknown organization, details should be collected otherwise the interrogee shall have the advantage. Knowledge about the current security scenario vis-a-vis the spurt of terrorist activities in the area may facilitate prolonging dialogue. Where details are not available, the specialized section in the Intelligence Bureau, R&AW, CBI etc may be requisitioned.

The core components of any terrorist outfit are youths and students. Interrogator must know how to tackle them. This category of subject may require prolonged and consequential persuasion. They may be amenable to logic and sustained reasoning. The solidarity and conviction of these youths are more or less limited to brainwashing done and thrusting an idea or dogma upon them. The experienced interrogators effort should remain to erase these pre-fixed ideology, self-designed ideas and dogmatism.They require soft handling. Psychological approach and ready wits of the interrogators are essential components. At no point of time muscle power be reflected on them. Another constraint is the knowledge about the laws governing these subjects. There are many special laws, acts and provisions under which these subjects can easily be booked. The process may also be different. The interrogators should have knowledge about these laws, both national and international. Often for obtaining feedback about a subject, INTERPOL may be consulted as the subject may be wanted in their record. Similarly other states should also require to be shared about the arrest with a view to ascertaining any case reference from them. This should be done without consuming any time and on top priority basis. It has been found that a subject arrested in a minor involvement might be a most wanted criminal in other cases. Foreigners are required to be dealt as per the laid down provisions.

Women subjects under this category often pose problems for want of interrogation-trained lady police officers. It remains a fact that women have had their triumphant role in terrorism. Their activities are not only confined to the areas of propaganda, liaison, communication, collection of funds, logistic supports, but a sizeable section, of late, is found taking active part in terror operations. Many of them have undergone arms training. Both in national and international terrorism theatre the revolutionary involvement and contributions of the women subjected them to inhuman torture, oppression, elimination and jail term. In India we have noticed the part played by women cadres / members of various militant outfits including the ULFA, BODO, LTTE, Dukhtaran-e-Millat (Daughters of Islam), Muslim Khawateen Markaz (Muslim Women's Centre) etc. Nalini (LTTE), Pranati Barua (ULFA), Ayesha Andrabi (DeM) are a few women who have registered their place in their respective organizations. Many organizations have their women cell too. The radical and extremist outfits have considerable women cadres. This obstacle can only be removed by providing training to lady police officers in scientific interrogation techniques. Their services may be requisitioned as and when needed. In this context one cautionary part is that these trained lady interrogators should constantly update their knowledge and skill.

Another damaging part is the media. Now-a-days the electronic media coverage is not only damaging the investigation but also act as an advanced intelligence supplier to the terrorists. It has been observed that often the revelations made by the subject, who all are wanted in this case, what are the sequential actions/

steps the police is likely to adopt, the legal complication, etc. are aired obviously for the benefit of the outfit members. They do adopt precautionary measures. As a matter of rules and procedures, utter secrecy about the interrogation is required to be maintained for the interest of not only of the case but also on count of national security. Terrorist acts do harbour many complications. Interrogators must be refrained from opening their mouth for the press-corps. Erring officials should be taken to task.

Language is another hindrance. It may be national or international. In case a subject speaks the language of another state, the action may be easy by summoning any officer from that particular state or any officer available in the police force acquainted with the spoken language of the subject. The maximum problem and time consuming factor orbit in the cases of foreign nationals, the language expert of which are not readily available. In such cases with the permission of the Court, ministry of home affairs and ministry of external affairs are informed for arranging an interpreter.

As already explained many outfits have their own intelligence wings and many members are trained in intelligence tradecraft. They are being taught about interrogation procedures. An Inter Services Intelligence (ISI/Pakistan) trained terrorist, during the course of interrogation, revealed what all he was taught about interrogation tradecraft adopted in India in a training centre in Pakistan. Interrogation is a battle of wits and thus the supremacy will be determined by the experience and tactfulness of the interrogator by outwitting his subject.

Interrogators should pay proper attention towards each and every word uttered by his subject. Terrorists have their own vocabularies and cue may be obtained from their utterings.

Item wise examination of the recoveries specially the telephone numbers and addresses recovered from the subject, are must. Let the subject explain each of them. Similarly small Tele tale evidences must also be scrutinized. In one case a tailor marking of a Pakistani in a shirt and in another case an airlines travel tag cornered the subject and he revealed his Pakistan visit. In another case a pocket Quran printed in Pakistan recovered from a subject broke his prolonged silence. In another case an Indian national working for an alien country was cornered owing to possession of a liquor bottle marked "for defence services only" provided to him by one of his cultivated source in the Army.

On the spot interrogation of the subject is very significant. The suspect remains in a shock and bewilderment. Positions of his group members/accomplices, arms-ammunition catche, escape route, further actions/targets, hideouts, communication modes, etc. are immediate requirement. It is necessary to protect these revelations from leakage and to orient immediate follow up actions.

Another cautionary part is to ensure physical secrecy and safety of the subject. He remains a target of his own group who want to silence him to plug any disclosure. While carrying an interrogation, this aspect may be kept in mind. The involement of mole in the police organization also cannot be ruled out. In every stage the corroborations of the revelations made are essential to gauge truthfulness.

12 Interrogation of Narco Offence-related Subjects

The post war years, along with the growth of terrorism, has witnessed emergence of drug trafficking as a global phenomenon with high destabilization capability. Over the time, international drug trafficking, which is the world's highest generation of liquidity outside government control, is intricately interlinked with terrorism. This aspect finally gave birth to narco-terrorism, a phenomenon promoting enormous security implications. The term "narco-terrorism" could be defined as the nexus between narcotic smuggling and terrorists with a view to generating funds for procuring arms-ammunition-explosives and also for augmenting other supports including liquid money to the latter to further their objectives. This nexus accentuated much seriousness now. Narcoterrorism has developed potentiality of destroying the social, economic and political fabrics of several nations and the security of some States is also under severe threat. It has also posed acute pressure and a formidable challenge even to the legally established order. The manufacture and delivery of narcotics became a part of terrorist portfolio for various reasons namely as a source of revenue generation to escalate their activities, to erode credibility of the opponents in all fronts, weakening the moral fabric of the target area people, enervating law enforcers, sponsoring organize crime networking and unrolling 'drugs for arms' transactions. The culture and seriousness of this very menace not only threatened the economy of the nation but also tolled upon the political, social and cultural fabric of the country. The police and other security agencies including the Narcotic Control Bureau of India, the nodal agency, are engaged in developing means and measures to control and thwart this menace by any means. The growing spurts and inter-linkages, accumulation of money, apart from faster communication modes are other alarming phenomenon. The integrity, stability, sovereignty and national health of the country besides economy, law and order, tranquility and prosperity etc. are intimately connected with it. The effect of narco-terrorism in this sub-continent is other interesting matter. The geo-politicians-underworld elements and most importantly connivance of some neighbouring States, promoting a serious challenge. Therefore, drug trafficking and drug abuse are two alarming menaces which require iron handling.

Illicit tracfficking in drugs generates unprecedented profits and has strong linkage with money laundering and financing of terrorist related criminal acts and activities, both nationally and internationally. This threat to the society needs to be tackled and aggressively countered with firm determination and urge. Addiction to narcotics and drugs is now recognized globally as one of the real dangers endangering mankind. The greed for easy monetary earnings through the sale of drugs, is considered as the worst form of organized crime. Narcotics interdiction, successful prosecution of drug traffickers and annihilation of the organized drug trafficking syndicates, besides awareness campaigning are a few tasks endorsed to the enforcing agencies.

The intelligence and security agencies per se, have been bestowed with these tasks and responsibilities to thwart this challenge by any means. The question of safeguarding national security should be the top priority. India's geographical position i.e. Golden Crescent in the west, Golden Triangle in the east, Nepal in the north, and the very porous natured border almost all around, are matters of grave anxiety. The country is badly affected by the terrorist militant/insurgent/extremist activities both of indigenous and foreign origin. Danger lies with the fact that these drug mafias and syndicate are capable of doing and undoing any criminal assault in any opportune moment. Another pertinent point is unfolding the hard criminal and the under world elements besides winning the favours of the corrupt and unpatriotic politicians. Clandestine relationship with the intelligence agencies too is added pressure. A study published by the *Executive Intelligence Review*, a private US Organization, revealed that where there is terrorism, there is usually a drug connection. On the other hand the terrorists often collect "protection money" from the drug smugglers as well. Drugs are used for years as a medicine purposes and for pleasure. Overdoses and continuous consumptions badly affect both the human physique and psyche. The drug abuse, therefore, is viewed a very serious threat to the society, especially to the youths.

Drug production and trafficking are new-fangled variations of terrorist modus operandi. It has gone global not confined to Afghanistan and Myanmar only. The escalation and rampant growth of narcotics trading has given rise to illegal arms-ammunition-explosive transshipments in favour of the terrorists/militants and in a few cases direct or indirect connivance of the State could also be traced.

Narcotic drug can be defined as a drug which in therapeutic doses diminishes awareness of sensory impulses, especially pain, by the brain. In large doses it causes stupor (condition of insensibility), coma or convulsions. In other words, a drug is any substance that can cause a change in human-body or way of thinking and feeling. Narcotic drugs would include:

1. Cannabis preparations like Bhang, Ganja, and Charas
2. Opium and alkaloids like morphine.
3. Coca alkaloids like Cocaine. and
4. Synthetic narcotic drugs like Pethidine.

ROUTES

Geographically India is sandwiched between two major sources of illicit drugs, the Golden Crescent comprising Pakistan, Afghanistan and Iran and the Golden Triangle comprising Myanmar, Thailand and Laos. Nepal is also a traditional source of Cannabis, both herbal and resinous. Illicit cultivation of Cannabis and Opium are also traced in various parts of the country specially in the areas of Chakrata and Uttarkashi in Uttarakhand, and Arunachal, Manipur, Nagaland in the North East, Idukki district in Kerala, Kodaikanal area of Tamil Nadu besides parts of Andhra Pradesh and West Bengal. However, there is an elaborate security system in both the opium factories at Neemuch in MP and Ghaziabad in UP to safeguard the stocks of opium kept in these factories.

LEGAL ASPECTS

In India, the legal arrangements are in full conformity with the three UN Conventions of 1961, 1971 and 1988 which together covered total number of 200 drugs and substances of abuse. The legal classification of about 200 substances into narcotic drugs and psychotropic substances is presumed to be the result of a historical process of development of international and national regulation and control starting from the Hague Convention of 1911. These substances have been classified into sedatives, tranquillizers, barbiturates, hallucinogens, stimulants and a few have also been categorized as "essential for medical use". The strategy devised to combat the menaces is four folded, namely regulatory, prohibited, preventive and curative. The attacks may be made at the production as well as consumption levels. Both the supply and the demand lines required to be duduced. The legal infrastructure for drug abuse control in India is rational but complex in nature.

The need for a national law and a common strategy applicable to the entire country, the Narcotic Drugs and Psychotropic Substance Act (NDPS Act) came into force w.e.f. 14.11.1985. This Act replaced the two old Opium Acts of 1857 and 1878 and the Dangerous Drugs Act of 1930. It superseded all State enactments on the subject too. The Act was further strengthened by a supplementary legislation for preventive detention in 1988. In 1989 another amendment was made on panel and procedural provisions. The Act provided extensive powers for making statutory rules to the Central and state government. It has left enough scope for making grounds for mobilizing voluntary nongovernment efforts in order to educating and curbing these menaces. Prevention, creation of public awareness, counseling, rehabilitation, social reintegration of the drug addicts have been placed under the Ministry of Welfare as well. The Act has further specified strict procedure for bails and expedites trial of the offender. For most of the offences the minimum punishment is 10 years RI and fine of Rupees one lac and these may be extended to 20 years RI and fine of Rupees Two lakh only. For a second time offence of certain serious natured, death penalty has been prescribed and for less offence, the punishment is 30 years RI and fine Rupees three lakh. The prescribed licensing authorities i.e. the Narcotic Commissioner of the Government of India and the Controller ot Drugs of all the States and UTs are also responsible for detection and investigation of contraventions and therefore have full policing functions in respect of all substances of abuse. Sections 41-51 of the Act, constitute a major departure from the Cr. P.C. where pre-registration powers of all selected agencies including the police, are to be authorized by notification

In exercise of the power given by the Act, the NCB was launched, being Delhi as Headquarters, on 17 March, 1986 precisely with the following powers and functioning:

Coordination of actions with various authorities under the NDPS Act, the Customs Act, the Drugs and Cosmetic Act, 1940 and other laws promulgated in this respect.

Implementation of the obligation in respect of counter measures against illicit traffic under the various international conventions and protocols that are in force at present or which may be ratified or acceded to by India in future.

Assistance to concerned authorities in foreign countries and concerned international organizations to facilitate coordination and universal action for prevention and suppression of illicit traffic of these drugs and substances and coordination of actions taken by other ministries, departments and organizations in respect of matters relating to drug abuse.

The NCB is the apex coordinating agency. Besides coordination and enforcement, the agency strives to promote inter-agency coordination with foreign countries, implement provisions of various international conventions, relating to drug abuse and illegal trafficking, liaison with international agencies like INTERPOL, Customs Cooperation Council, H.M. Customs and Excise of U.K., Drug Enforcement Agency of the USA, RCMP of Canada, RILO, Hong Kong, SAARC and enforcement agencies of other countries. Another significant task carried out by the NCB is the role played in keeping tracks with the dedicated special calls for narcotics launched by many States. Not only the police force but also the agencies like the BSF, CRPF, Coast Guards, Customs, Economic Intelligence Bureau, CBI are other few organizations with whom the NCB discharged joint responsibilities, when demanded. Imparting of training is another important function carried out by the NCB. In this sojourn, the USA is often a partner.

NEXUS BETWEEN TERRORISTS AND NARCO TRADERS

The unholy alliance between the terrorists/anti – social elements and the drug barons/ syndicates, became a serious upcoming problem, resulting into phenomenal spurt of militant activities and acts. This alliance not only threatened the integrity, security and stability of the country but also affected the social fabrics of the society. There are many instances to expose the connection and connivance of the Punjab, Kashmir and North East outfits with this nefarious designs. International linkages and inroads into the underworld heartlands, courtesy the ISI and Pakistan's endeavour radically changed the security scenario. This phenomenon is a matter of special worry to a developing country like ours.

INTELLIGENCE GENERATION

Collection of hard and actionable intelligence is a much sought after area owing to underground and clandestine nature of operation. Moreover the drug barons are influential people and they are also known for their muscle powers. The term intelligence may be defined as, "collection of accurate, up-to-date, and relevant information without the knowledge of the target in all fields of interest by the government agency for the use of the government for action at any time". As we are aware, there are only six sources of intelligence collection viz. agents, secret enquiries, interrogation, surveillance and interception and observation. In order to cover narcotic trafficking all these six sources may be employed.

INTERROGATION

In the investigation process interrogation plays a pivotal role. In order to unearth many hidden information which cannot be obtained through other means, the subjects are either interviewed or interrogated. In the case of Narco related offences since both the kingpins and the peddlers are diehard criminals, they may not be easily subjugated. The lure of money and the fear of elimination are also negative factors. Inspite of all these odds, systematic and detailed interrogation should be initiated, soon after the apprehension. Prior to taking up interrogation, through personal search and also examination of all the seized items are mandatory. All the prescribed norms and techniques of scientific interrogation, as discussed in earlier chapters, are also applicable subject to the need of the case. Planning and preparations and specially chalking out of the probable questions have heavy bearing on the outcome. It is important in a drug related interrogation to make proper effort to establish the chain and linkages. Rapport building with the interrogee is a must. Initially, crime context and punishment factors may not be touched. Creating an urge to speak the truth is an essential element. It is better to continue with the dialect spoken and understood by the subject. Battle of wits, appropriate approach and systematically advancing may help in creating confidence in the mind of the subject. Strong determination must be there. Never put any leading question. The cover story put forward by the subject may be hard to crack. The extent of the involvement of the subject is to be determined. The final destination of the substances and the end users are most important aspects. Body language and non-verbal communications should be observed and analyzed by the interrogating team. Do not forget to take photograph, finger prints and specimen signature besides other requirements. Choose the weakest one first in case of more arrests.

Subjects of interrogation may be:

Drug barons/lords/gang stars.

Foreigners.

Underground elements.

Veteran criminals.

Border touts.

Professional smugglers.

Women.

Children.

Terrorists/Militants/Anti-national elements.

Members of the diplomatic missions and other such privileged persons.

White collar criminals.

Drug addicts. Victims.

Repeated foreign travelers/visitors. Courier agency employees.

Unearthing the damage done and making proper assessment thereon, are done through interrogation. Both national security aspect and the social factor are equally important. Initiation of a case is important but more important is eradication and thwarting of the menace. Reward provocation may tempt the informants, even officials, to paddle the substance and concoct a case, of which interrogators should be cautious enough. To unearth the truth is the goal. All other temptations must be buried. The revelations made are always vetted. Attention is automatically focused on important points but the so-called unimportant revelations too are required to be noted for further probe. Secrecy of the revelation made is of paramount importance. These need to be well guarded. Press and media may be kept out of purview. Actionable inputs need to be perused without consuming time. In the age of faster communication mode, delay in action may go in favour of the perpetrators. It may be kept in mind that the syndicate managers have their own intelligence networking. In the case of arrest of foreigner, the instructions in this regards should be abided by. Joint interrogation involving the concerned agencies may produce good dividend. In this case, proper coordination, team cohesion and putting up the only trained interrogators are needed. Most of the drug trafficking organizations have a complex structure with a series of buffers.This arrangement is difficult to expose as the interrogee may be able to name only his contact persons. The interrogators must have patience and they have to knit the entire case through other modes of investigations. Another hindrance is out of jurisdiction and even out of country connections. As already pointed out to combat this particular offence there are many designated agencies and bodies. Interrogators should be well abreast of all these formations and these need to be consulted promptly. Emanation of actionable inputs as early as possible may be the motto. The fear and inhibitions prevailing in the mind of the subject need to be erased and confidence may be built. The interrogation room effect can not be ignored. Initially the subject may be given a patient hearing. His each uttering should be given proper attention and he may be allowed to speak. The more he will speak, the more contradictions may arise. The witty interrogators always make notes of all these contradictions and the subject is questioned on these points and finally he is broken. Undercover operators are more dangerous as they produce documents in their favour. All those needed in this process of investigation include determination, strong will, professional competency, training, experience, up-dated knowledge, honesty, and commendable personality.

13 Interrogation of Subjects connected with Economic Offences

Economic offences are not a new phenomenon. The crime world is meddled with the offences committed under this head. Economic offences form a separate category owing to very nature and crime content. These are often referred to as white/blue collar crimes committed by technocrats, reputed businessmen, highly qualified individuals, corporate magnets, well connected people, corrupt public servants, and political bigwigs. In economic offences not only individuals get victimized suffering pecuniary loss, but such crimes also affect the very fabric of the national security as well. The offences like trafficking of narcotic substances, pumping of fake/counterfeiting currencies, financial scams and bank frauds, evoke serious impact on national security and governance.

The Central Economic Intelligence Bureau was set up in July, 1985 with the main objective of coordinating and strengthening the intelligence gathering activities, the investigative efforts and enforcement action by various agencies concerned with investigation into economic offences and enforcement of economic laws. The Bureau was made responsible for proper coordination, liaison, guidance, control as well as providing directions to the concerned departments both at the Central and State level. The charter of tasking included:

- Collection of intelligence relating to black economy and conduction of in-depth investigation there on.

- Keeping watch on different aspects of economic offences and emergence of new types of such offences and also to evolve counter measures required for effective annihilation of these threats.
- To undertake investigative studies, and
- Preparation of a monthly bulletin indicating latest trends.
- And conduction of trainings.

Economic offences may be either cognizable or non-cognizable in nature. Local police normally deal with cheating, counterfeiting, criminal breach of trust related offences. They are now heavily burdened with various kinds of frauds, evasions, scams, and also cyber related crimes. The police have to assist other agencies too like the CBI, Narcotic Control Bureau, Central Board of Direct Taxes. Collectors of Customs, Collectors of Central Excise, Directorate of Enforcement, Directorate General of Foreign Trade, Anti Corruption Bureau, Central Vigilance Commission and any other State wings dealing with these offences.

Offences under this head are many. Few are mentioned below:

Tax evasions.

Banking and postal frauds

Money laundering.

Foreign exchange racketing. Foreign contribution manipulation.

Hawala operations.

Smuggling/illicit trafficking in contraband goods.

Price fixing

Bid rigging.

Counterfeiting of govt. stamps.

Adulteration. Illicit drug trafficking.

Bribing and corruption of public servants.

Black-marketing and hoarding.

Criminal misappropriation.

Criminal breach of trust.

Cheating

Forgery.

Narcotic trading.

FICN (Fake Indian Currencies Note)

Insurance frauds. Share market and stock exchange scams.

Intellectual Property Crimes.

Evasion of excise duty.

Cultural object's theft.

Fraudulent bankruptcy.

Bank frauds.

Racketeering in employment.

Illegal foreign trade.

Narco trafficking.

Illicit trafficking in arms.

Cyber crime/Computer crime.

The interrogation of the economic crime offenders are normally entrusted to the experienced and trained hands. The reasons are many, namely (1) gravity of the offence, (2) quantum of loss, (3) pressure mounted by the senior official formation, (4) criticism of the public, (5) outcry of the press and media, (6) craftiness of the offence, (7) political pressure (8) involvement of terrorists/militants, (9) chasing of the party concerned and (10) keeping the prestige of the police organization. Many a time, the question of national security is in jeopardy. The quantum of loss and going of the booty in wrong hands, often are matters of grave concern. Transnational involvement may also affect diplomatic relationships. Other nations may also evince their interest in the detection and thwarting endeavours. The entire globe is serious about drug peddling. The USA put their officers in each of their important diplomatic missions in order to liaise with the concerned state in dealing with illegal drug trading. The economic offenders are nevertheless criminals but they differ from other criminals on many counts like motive and intention, team efforts, craftmanship and proper planning, scientific bend of mind, good homework done, accurate intelligence generation, secrecy of the operation, carrying out dry run, adoption of new techniques, observation of need to know principle, raising of sources in the target area, speedy communication networking and using of codes, utilization of the organized gangs and underworld elements, patronage of the state and intelligence agencies, influence beyond borders, mobility, neo-modus operandi, local base, enduse of the gained amount, political patronage and pan world linkages. Another vital aspect is limited sphere of knowledge of the interrogee as he remains orbited within his tasking and area. Offences like drug peddling, hawala operation, smuggling, money laundering, foreign exchange racketing, FICN pumping, intellectual property crime, smuggling of antics, etc do follow a pattern in which cutouts are used in order to keep the chain of operation unexposed. In case of any interception in the chain it becomes difficult to expose the chain of command. The couriers can only reveal the name of the person from whom they received the item and the point of termination. The beauty of the operation is such that pseudo names are used to evade police dragnet. Annihilation of the agents in the event of their apprehension may also be kept in mind. Therefore, proper guarding and adequate security measures of the interrogees are required to be streamlined.

The role of the interrogators in carrying out this job is engulfed with tactness, approach, experience, knowledge, personality and professional competency. In average cases, pressure is a likely fallout owing to involvement of the bigwigs. The undermentioned points need to be covered depending upon the compatibility of the case :

(a) Proper identification of the interrogee and fixing his address.

(b) Photograph should be taken. If needed, the same may be circulated, nationally and internationally including INTERPOL.

(c) Intent/motive of the crime may be ascertained.

(d) Exposing of the operation net is a must.

(e) Recruitment process and training. Motivation angle.

(f) Communication channels used. Cellphone numbers.

(g) Codes/signs/cryptology used.

(h) Method of identification of the receivers.

(i) Nexus with other gangs, politicians, police, administration.

(j) In case of organized gang, details of the same.

(k) Transnational linkages.

(l) Existence of moles in the target. Ascertaining of the details thereon.

(m) Local supports.

(n) Gang composition.

(o) Arms holdings.

(p) Kingpins.

(q) Harbourers.

(r) Modus operandi adopted.

(s) Future targets.

(t) Criminalization in the group/organization.

(u) Strength and identification of the members.

(v) Receiver of stolen properties.

(w) Pocket of influence.

(x) Past crimes conducted/within his knowledge.

(y) Fronts opened.

(z) Location of the operation points, printing presses, offices, godowns, stocking centers, laboratories, computer centers, etc.

The undermentioned points may also be kept in view:

(a) The individuals involved in these crimes are people of shady characters. Therefore their revelations need to be vetted before adopting conclusions.

(b) The cover story revealed by them may not be trusted without verification.

(c) Many of the apprehended persons are afraid of retaliatory actions by the outfit. This may be erased from their mind.

(d) Proper follow up of the revelations are must and these should be conducted without consuming much time. Secrecy of the revelations are desired norms.

(e) Frisking of the person and the recoveries made are must at the very outset.

(f) Prompt interrogation may provide good dividend. Later on the interrogee may be tutored.

(g) Never allow any unauthorized staff member, even other seniors, privy to the disclosures till culmination of the case.

(h) Endeavour should be to collect as much hard evidences as possible.

(i) Your effort may also be oriented towards cultivation of sources (agents).

(j) Never try without planning and preparation. Checking of past records and even consultation with other agencies be carried.

(k) Take note of total revelations, in verbatim, you may initially not be posted with the fact. Anything new should further be corroborated.

(l) Keep the press, media and unauthorised persons away till the culmination of the case for security reason.

Bibliography

Fundamental of Criminal Investigation By Charles O'Hara

Police Investigation By John Walkley

Criminal Investigation By Arthur S. Aurby

Modern Criminal Investigation By Harry Sodderman & John O'Connel

Principles of Police Investigation By C.H.Van Meter.

Principles of Criminal Law & Investigation (Part 1&2) By R. Deb

Field Interrogation By Allen P Bristow and Charles C Thomas

Effective Interviewing and Interrogation Techniques By Nothan J Gordon and William L Fleisher

Principle and Procedures of the Art of Cross Examination By P. Ramanathan Aiyar & P Raghava Aiyar

Secrets of Mind Power By Harry Lorayne

The Penguin Book of Interviews Edited By Christopher Silverter

Principles of Kinesic Interview and Interrogation By Stan B Walters

Beyond Breaking Point By Peter Deeley

Kautilya's Arthasastra Translated by Rudrapatna Shamashastry

Women, Crime And Criminology, A Feminist Critique By Carol Smart

Violence Against Women Edited by K Uma Devi

Crime Against Women By Ram Ahuja

The Juvenile Justice System of India By Ved Kumari

Women and Crime By S.K. Ghosh

Sex Crimes By Terry Thomas

Genetics and DNA Technology: Legal Aspects By Wilson Wall

Introduction to Forensic Sciences By William G Eckert

Crime Against Women and Protective Laws By Shobha Saxena

Constitution of India By DD Basu

Constitution of India By Shukla and Sen

Constitutional Remedies and Writs By Durga Das Basu

Naxalism : Causes and Cure By P.K. Agrawal

Human Rights and Police By Padmashri Dr S Subramanian

Criminal Manual By Justice Khastagir

Drug Enforcement Training Manual, United Nations

Drug Law Enforcement Training Compendium, Narcotic Control Bureau, New Dilhi.

Terrorism and Drugs By Sankar Sen

Global Drug Enforcement By Gregory D Lee

Narco Terrorism By Giriraj Shah & RC Dikshit

Drug Interdiction By George S Steffen & Samual M Chandelaria

Intelligence Imperatives for India By D C Nath

How to Recognize and Handle Abnormal People By Robert A Matthews and Loyd W Rowland

Terrorists in India By Charles Tegart

Global Terrorism By Harry Henderson

Terrorism: World Under Siege By S K Ghosh

Bio Terrorism & Bio Defence By P R Chari & Suba Chandran

Criminology By Ahmed Siddique

Organised Crime By C K Gandhirajan

Terrorism & Organised Crime By Ram Gopal Verma

Left Extremist Movements in West Bengal By A K Samanta

Towards Naxalbari By Pradip Basu

The Naxalite Movement By Sankar Ghosh

The Naxalite Movement By Biplav DasGupta

Maoist Spring Thunder By Arun Prosad Mukherjee

Naxalbari—is not just the name of a village By Chandan Roy

Documents of the History of the Communist Party of India Edited by G Adhikari

Bharater Communist Andolaner Aro Kichu Grathabali (Bengali) By Harinarayan Adhikari

A Text Book of Psychology By P N Bhattacharyya

Police and Politics in India By Kripal Dhillon

Ragged War By Leory Thomson

Islam and Modern Histroy By W C Smith

Principles of Mohammedan Law By Mulla

Jane's Intelligence (March, 2003)

Corporate Crimes By Prakash Talwar

Frauds and Financial Crimes in Cyber Space By Yogesh Barua

Transnational Criminal Organizations and Money Laundering By James R Richards

Indian Banking—Crime and Security in Indian Banks By S K Ghosh

Economic Offences By S K Ghosh

Money Launders By Robert E Powis

Index